Outwitting Writer's Bl

and Other Problems of the Pen

Jenna Glatzer

Series Concept Created by Bill Adler, Jr.

THE LYONS PRESS

Guilford, Connecticut
An imprint of The Globe Pequot Press

Books by Jenna Glatzer:

Exploration of the Moon
Native American Festivals and Ceremonies
Taking Down Syndrome to School
Conquering Panic and Anxiety Disorders
Words You Thought *You Knew*

The Lyons Press is an imprint of The Globe Pequot Press.

10 9 8 7 6 5 4 3 2

Printed in the United States of America

Designed by Compset, Inc.

ISBN 1–59228–124–9

Library of Congress Cataloging-in-Publication Data is available on file.

OUTWITTING is a trademark of Adler and Robin Books, Inc., and is licensed to Lyons Press, Inc., and its permitted licensees for use with this series. The concept for the series was created by Bill Adler, Jr.

Acknowledgments

More than any other book I've written, this one has been a collaborative effort. I owe a big debt of gratitude to Rusty Fischer, whose input is all over this book, as well as my two writing groups: the Screenplayers (www.screenplayers.net) and the Net Wits (www.thenetwits.com), for their valuable feedback. Within these groups I especially want to thank Pete Barnstrom, Robin Reed, Mary J. Schirmer, and Irv Eisenberg. Double-big thanks to Bill Harper (www.humourwriter.com), one of the funniest writers I know, for his terrific feedback and zingers.

And I couldn't have written this without all of the inspiration I get from the 73,000 wonderful subscribers to my online writers' magazine, Absolute Write (www.absolutewrite.com).

I thank Djana Pearson Morris for her confidence in me, Bill Adler, Jr. for creating this series, The Lyons Press for choosing me to write this book, and my editor, Lilly Golden, for her insight and wisdom.

For Anthony Policastro, who complained very rarely and even made me pasta while I was carrying on an affair with my computer during the making of this book.

Table of Contents

Know Your Enemy

1

W riter's block is an insidious pest—a beady-eyed rodent hiding under the floorboards of even the hardest working writers, waiting to rear its hideous head at the most inopportune times.

If you've ever found yourself staring at the blank page all day or cleaning out the refrigerator for the fifth time in a week (is that cottage cheese or spinach dip?), just to avoid being taunted by that blasted blinking cursor, then you've experienced writer's block.

The good news? It means you're a writer. Find me a writer—famous or otherwise—who has never had an off day, and I'll show you a writer who has pungent body odor and abnormally hairy toes.

It's not important that you have these times; what's important is how you deal with them. You can give in and sort your frozen vegetables according to how far your children will spit them out, or you can be a Real Writer and work through the block until you're back to your regular brilliant self.

The battle lines are drawn, the stage is set, the choice is yours: draw out your crossbow and battle the beast, or hide

1

behind the sacrificial virgin in the white dress currently chained between two posts and wait for the inevitable to happen.

A nasty case of "writus interruptus" can truly stop you in your tracks. The variables are how you react, and what choices you make, conscious or unconscious, to actively make writer's block a thing of the past.

Tools to Fight the Block

When writer's block is chronic, it's like having a work-related injury without the benefit of disability insurance or the all-important company get-well card. I have yet to meet a writer who's successfully convinced an editor to compensate her for time off to recover from brain strain. Therefore, it's important to build up the tools to learn how to bounce back—quickly and effectively—from a paralyzed pen.

Some of those tools include:

- Letting your idea percolate
- Learning to silence the inner critic
- Free writing
- Relaxation techniques
- Changing the fundamentals of your fiction, like the sex of your main character, or the setting of your story
- Getting feedback from other writers
- "Borrowing" material from other writers
- Setting your own deadline and learning better time-management skills

We'll talk about these and many other tools throughout this book.

Just as in any other twelve-step program, admitting you have a problem is the very first stage on the road to recovery. Fortunately, the second step doesn't involve announcing your name and condition in front of a room full of strangers.

Define the Cause

Your problem may be coming from a noisy inner critic (or an even noisier next-door neighbor), a story that you won't allow to come out and play, troubling life circumstances, insomnia, or myriad other things thrown in your path on this great obstacle course we call the writing life. Maybe you're afraid of failure or afraid of success. Maybe the voice of your father is ringing in your head: "Get a real job!" Maybe you haven't fully developed the story in your mind, so it won't miraculously appear on the page.

Even if you think your block came from "out of nowhere," you know—at least on a subconscious level—why you're blocked. Now it's time to become conscious of the cause and then work through it. "A funny thing happens to writer's block when you address it head-on," says author Kimberly Ripley. "It squirms when you look it in the face and demand some answers."

Writer's Block Is an Equal-Opportunity Offender

There are two reasons to write: for love and for money. The luckiest of us get to do it for both. Neither reason is any more important, highfalutin, morally correct, artistic, or real than the other. Just because your goal is to earn money from your writing doesn't make you a traitor to your art, just like never being paid (or even published) doesn't make you any less of a writer.

And writer's block can be just as devastating, regardless of your primary goal. Clearly, if you depend on your writing income to live, writer's block is a major problem. But it's also problematic if you write as therapy or for creative satisfaction. When I don't write, I feel sick. It's sort of the same feeling as having low blood sugar—I feel lethargic and incomplete, like I need my next fix. So, it's back to the keyboard for my mental candy bar.

If that candy bar's not there? Oh, the horror! I'm lost. I walk around, frazzled and dazed, forgetting where I put my sneakers and my elbows, hoping the sun will set sooner today so I can just get back to bed and be done with it. After all, tomorrow is bound to be a more productive day—right?

There are some awful people who claim to never get writer's block. More likely, they just intuitively know how to work through it and don't even realize they're doing it. Once you've practiced some coping strategies over and over, you don't have to consciously recognize that you're doing them anymore. It's a lot like walking. You had to learn to do it once upon a time, but it's surely been a long time since you've had to think about doing it (except, possibly, for the last office Christmas party). You get up, you do it; you don't think about it anymore.

That's the beauty of overcoming writer's block: the more you do it, the easier it gets. Until, one day, one beautiful, shining, glorious day, you too can be one of those awful people who crows, "I never get writer's block—anymore!"

▶ PROMPT: What did your character's mother tell her never to do? Write about the first time she broke that rule.

Unlearn Your School-Days Writing Lessons

Just as emotional eaters are formed by well-meaning mothers doling out just a little too much comfort food in times of youthful distress, writer's block can also be traced to our childhoods.

After all, from elementary school on, teachers—much like future editors—begin grading our writing, often on a daily basis. Talk about pressure!

Teachers, who are not necessarily good (or even decent) writers themselves, have their own systems for judging students' work. Most often, they have some sort of formula for determining a grade—perhaps in a "critical thinking" essay, Mrs. Morgan expected you to cover three main points and would give you up to 25 percent for the substance of each. Then there was 10 percent for spelling and grammar, 10 percent for neatness and presentation, and 5 percent for writing style. Although this kind of formula devalues a writer's craft, it is understandable. Answers must be right, no matter how well written they are. If the answer is "A," putting down the letter "B" is just plain wrong, even if you did fluff it up with a little Shakespearean dialect—"The answereth is foundeth in penning the letter B." But is it always black and white? Can all the answers be found in the teacher's manual? Shouldn't creativity count for *something*?

After all, what is writing, if not creativity? And what are our first opportunities at real writing in school? Book reports. Research papers. Interpretations. Forged absence notes from your mother. And with so much riding on these papers (especially those absence notes), what early writer *wouldn't* be stressed?

Yet usually, the quality of the writing played second fiddle to whether or not you covered the points the teacher wanted you to cover. And when a writer attempted to interpret something—usually the work of another writer—look out! I remember when one of my teachers told me I had interpreted Samuel Beckett all wrong. The wiseass in me wanted to ask her if, since she obviously had a telepathic connection with Mr. Beckett and could discern the single correct interpretation of Vladimir's line "I might have some turnips" in *Waiting For Godot*, she could also tell me what my cat was thinking when she defecated in my shoes instead of the litter box.

In fact, I rarely managed to interpret literary works "correctly." Some would say I thought too much; I never wanted to accept the simplest meanings of symbolism. To me, if a character wore sunglasses, it didn't mean he was a secretive person. It meant he was so sensitive that he was unable to face the rawness of the world. Either that, or the sun was bright that day. So, although I took honors English, my teacher once took me aside and told me I didn't have to take the advanced placement test at the end of the year, because she could tell who would do well and who wouldn't, and my writing wasn't up to par.

Listen to Yourself

For years, I took this teacher's word as gospel, and interpreted it to mean that I was not good enough to be a professional writer. I have yet to go back to my old high school and deposit a stack of my books and articles on her desk with a smirk (or a middle finger, depending on my mood), but it remains high on my list of temptations.

My father still talks about the teacher who humiliated him by making fun of his poem in front of the whole class because he used the words "silently speaking eyes." Now, as adults, you and I may wince at the cliché, but when you're a junior high school student, "silently speaking eyes" is pretty deep. He was a young boy trying to express his sensitive side through writing, and he got laughed at because of it.

And then there's that time your teacher downgraded you on your short story because "ain't *isn't* a word." Never mind the fact that you were just trying to be true to your character's voice. Never mind the fact that in third grade you were trying to use the word ain't as a symbol for America's growing lethargy and ennui as a superpower. Never mind the fact that the word ain't appears about five gazillion times in that *other* great American literary classic, *The Adventures of Huckleberry Finn*. It ain't fair, I tell ya!

Thus a battle with the blank page—and a recurring nightmare about chalk dust and red pens—begins. If you've ever had a similar experience, you probably understand how deeply a teacher's words can sting. But now that you're an adult, you get to redefine yourself. What you love is what you are meant to do. Period. If you love writing, then you are meant to write. It doesn't matter what your teacher said, or failed to say. Listen to yourself. That teacher no longer has any power over your life, and you get to accept or reject her opinions now. I want you to ask yourself if you are meant to write. If the answer is "yes," then no teacher can stop you anymore. It's up to you to motivate yourself and live up to your potential.

Your Beautiful Blank Canvas

I ask you, what's so bad about a blank page? When did the words "blank page" become synonymous with the writer's version of premature balding?

Rather than seeing the blank page as your sworn enemy, learn to see it as the beautiful blank canvas it is. The marks you make on it don't have to be perfect, and they don't have to be permanent. You can cross out, press the delete key, toss them out, or set them on fire when you're done—but every mark you make is progress.

The blank page is your place to play, invent new worlds, work out your anger, meditate, ruminate, vent, show off, and capture memories. But mostly play.

Unlike back in grade school, you are now writing because you *choose* to. Announcement: writing is now optional!

Love the Labor

There's something to be said for stick-to-it-iveness and discipline, but there's also something to be said for enjoying every aspect of your life. Presumably, you started writing because you derived some satisfaction from it. Dare I say you enjoyed it? (I dare.)

Do you enjoy it now? Aside from the block, that is. If the unblocking fairy came down and visited you tomorrow, what would your life look like? Would you be happy while you're writing? Not just afterward, but in the act itself.

Writing, unlike many other careers, is a labor of love. A host of other careers offer more glamour, popularity, concrete results, security, opportunities to meet hot members of the opposite sex, and above all, a steadier paycheck. Yet thousands join the writers' fold each year.

Is it because we enjoy losing our eyesight by the age of forty? Because getting high on inkjet printer fumes takes us back to the '60s? Are we obsessed with the clicking sound our keyboards make? Or are we, perhaps, overly fond of licking postage stamps, only to wait by the mailbox for days, weeks, and months on end for (yet another) letter that includes the words "does not meet our needs at this time?"

Chances are, not so much. We love writing, and would do it even if it meant losing our eyesight by thirty and getting twice as many rejection letters. Like monks who take a vow of silence or those daring souls who think it's perfectly natural to want to climb Mount Everest, writers are not made—they are *called.* (The mountain climbers, however, are called lunatics.) Called to the love of language, called to the lure of a brightly lit bookstore, called to Office Depot on a Friday night to check out the latest in padded 9-by-12-inch envelopes.

And so, being called, does it make any sense if we're *not* enjoying what we're doing?

▶ PROMPT: What would your character die for? Prove it.

Time for a Change

It's essential to take the time to step back and evaluate whether or not you're having any fun at what you do. If not, figure out why not. It doesn't mean you have to forget about writing altogether if you discover you're not digging it. It just means you have to try something different—a different genre, medium, approach, schedule, method for working, or just a new story. Maybe it's time to move to a new writing space, to write at different times of the day, or to write in color.

Maybe you've been writing too much lately, or perhaps not enough. Maybe you write more in the spring, less in the winter. Or vice versa. Maybe you're a morning writer, or an evening writer, and think you should be both. Maybe you don't write as much as the friends in your local writing group, or maybe you write more than they do, but still not "enough."

Writer's block isn't deadly. It isn't even contagious, although sometimes we may wish we could spread it, like a hacking cough, to those obnoxiously prolific people who claim they never get it. It's just a sign that it's time to change something. Think of it as an opportunity to experiment and delve into a new creative pursuit. "I remember something I learned in a tennis manual," says humor writer Bill Harper, "Never change a winning game plan, and always change a losing one."

Learning from the Block

The joy of overcoming writer's block is in turning a lose-lose situation into a win-win. Learning to cope with writer's block may just make you a better writer when you're *not* blocked. The tools you gain here, the lessons you learn, will not only equip you to better handle writer's block, but better handle being a writer altogether.

Many of us coast by on past experiences, past achievements, past stories, past publishing credits. We get stuck in a rut, turning out the same genre novels or filling the same pages of a scientific journal. And while there's nothing wrong with getting published anywhere, and even less wrong with getting paid, perhaps your current case of writer's block is really more a case of opportunity knocking and you having your radio turned up too loudly to hear it. Don't have a radio? Must be that blasted next-door neighbor again.

Writer's block is there to teach you something. You have to decide what lesson it's trying to give. At the core, writer's block is fear. Of what? You pick: of failure, of success, of losing yourself, of finding yourself, of not measuring up, of disappointing someone, of having to move to the next stage, of being egotistical, of discovering writing isn't going to complete your life, of neglecting your family, of missing a deadline, of being exposed as undereducated . . .

Fear. Big freakin' deal. You can handle a little fear. Yes, you can.

Not only can you handle it, but you can let it fuel you. You can turn that fear into excitement, and find out that deep down, you're an excellent risk taker. You wouldn't be a writer if you weren't a closet daredevil—the literary Evil Knievel, hopefully with fewer broken bones.

Daredevils write from their guts rather than their fingertips. That's you. A daredevil. So get used to it. It's not your fault. You were just born that way. Some people have blue eyes, some have freckles, and others have the power to take flying leaps off telephone poles with the astounding power of their words.

No matter how experienced or green you are, you are not immune to writer's block. But rather than fighting it or hiding from it, you can use it as an opportunity to learn more about yourself and your writing. Or you can stay blocked. It's your choice. (Pssst, c'mon, do it. All the cool kids are getting unblocked. Pity they still wear their baseball caps backward.)

To start your journey, just turn the page.

2

Start at the Very Beginning

If you're just starting out as a writer and you're already blocked, chances are that you're a bit frigid because you're unsure of your skills, or you're too caught up in believing that whatever you write has to be perfect. Surprise! Most of what first flies out of writers' fingers is sheer garbage.

The alphabet contains twenty-six letters. You, the Real Writer, just have to take those twenty-six letters and twist them around into a series of combinations that *eventually* make profound sense. Maybe just to you, or maybe for an audience. Like I said, neither goal is better than the other. I am actually more intrigued by the writers who don't care a whit about publication.

Most new writers seem to think that publication will somehow validate them and erase all their fears. They believe that the minute some faceless editor in New York deems their words worthy of killing trees, they will get a magic infusion of confidence and never dread the blank page again.

Publication Won't Erase the Block

Maybe now's not the best time to mention this, but I'm sadistic.

In college, one of my professors made us read a wonderful short story collection by Pam Houston: *Cowboys Are My Weakness.* Turns out that she was a former student of his, and the book got phenomenal reviews. She got compared to all kinds of famous writers—the kind of thing that should have given her a shot of egomania the size of Mars and infused her with zeal to return to her keyboard and type like heck. Instead, my professor mentioned offhandedly, the effusive praise hit her more like a fly ball in the eye; she was terrified to write another word, afraid she would never be able to live up to the reviewers' expectations. Now, she did write again, mind you, or I would never have told you this story. But publication didn't make her road easier—it made it harder—much like all the road improvement projects the government organizes.

Before publication, she was free to write whatever she liked, and if it went over, great—if not, she had no reputation to lose. Now there was more at stake.

Eventually, she had to find the nerve to take the risk and be a daredevil again, just like you. No matter what the reviews said, the next time she sat down to start a new story, it was just her and the blank page, and a whole world of doubt, possibility, and fun waiting to be had.

▶ PROMPT: Write as an eight-year-old. Not about an eight-year-old, but about a grown-up subject, from the point of view of yourself at eight years old.

Thinking Like an Artist

When I was in college, I began as an art major. I lived and breathed art, which played havoc with my hay fever. After sev-

eral classes, I started seeing the world as lights and darks, color
and shadow. I looked at a tree and envisioned which medium I
would choose to depict it—watercolor? Oil paint? Colored pencils? I regularly configured my fingers into a frame and looked
at my world through it, seeing the layout of the page. Seeing the
focal point, the background, the foreground. Not always seeing
the pole in front of me.

"That sky has such strong contrast," I said. "The white clouds
against the deep purple sunset; I can see it in oils."

"You really think like an artist," my friend Yoshi told me.

It's funny, though—when I switched career paths, I quit seeing
the world that way. Oh, there are still moments when I notice a de-
liciously ripe bit of scenery, or look at someone's clothing and
want to get out my best pen to ink the folds and curves. But I fail
to think like this during all of my waking hours the way I once did.

Again, it's a matter of learning and unlearning a habit.
When I was immersed in the art world, I thought like an artist.
When I got out of the art world, I slowly unlearned those habits
that felt instinctual at the time. It took longer for me to start
thinking like a writer.

Seeing Through Writer's Eyes

Seeing the world as an artist is perhaps easier; it's training our
eye to see things as complete pictures. Training yourself to "see
things visually" is redundant. Seeing the world as a writer means
looking at things and seeing words and metaphors instead.

It means looking at a woman in a grocery store and seeing,
"She was as warm and inviting as a fresh-baked cookie, and just
as likely to fall apart." It means looking at a traffic light and seeing an extended metaphor about the changing of—*Beep*. Oh,
pardon me, the light turned green.

See the world through writer's eyes. I challenge you. Just don't do it at traffic lights.

When you write, you bring to the table all of your perceptions and life experiences. It will be much easier for you to get them down on paper if you've already translated them into words.

Exercise:

Right now, I want you to look around you and tell me what you see, through writer's eyes. I want to read all about your desk, your bedroom, your pet, your food, yourself. I want to hear what you're seeing right now in words.

You don't need a lot of flowery adjectives. Adjectives are like fine chocolate; they're best savored in small pieces. Don't try to gobble down that whole box of chocolates at once, just bite off a small bit and taste how thick with flavor it is. And then send me the rest—I love chocolate.

Strong nouns, strong verbs. Hear the echo of every good writing instructor in America. Tell me about the computer that should have applied for disability benefits last year. Tell me about the stuffed animal whose missing ear was loved off it.

When you go out, take in all the sensations through your writer's senses. Define that smell. Don't tell me it smells musty— tell me it smells like your old camp bag after you stored wet bathing suits in it all summer.

See a woman as a poem and a beach as a short story. See an injustice as an article, a broken (then mended) heart as a novel.

Make These Moments Happen

While you undoubtedly have these moments from time to time, you can make them happen more often just by intending for them to happen rather than walking around passively hoping the muse will come along sometime.

Don't expect these revelations to hit you by magic. Practice consciously evoking them. Take trips just to practice opening your writer's eyes.

Keep a small notebook or tape recorder handy so that when you come across a particularly brilliant insight or phrase, you can record it for later use.

Although I started thinking like a writer without truly meaning to do so, I didn't experience this nearly-around-the-clock writer perception until I started doing it on purpose. You have to mean for it to happen, and do it even when it doesn't feel natural.

This is how you can become the conduit through which great writing flows; practice thinking like a writer all the time, and then when you want to call upon your skills, you'll be more than ready for the challenge.

Keep your perceptions sharp (not to mention your pencil), and force yourself to define things in words. Make yourself be specific; challenge yourself to find the best possible words to define a particular person, event, sound, and so on.

I'm always amused when a writer says, "I just can't describe how beautiful it was," or "words can't express how much you mean to me." That's your job—to describe how beautiful it was, and to use words to express how much she means to you. If not a writer, then who else?

There is no better antidote to writer's block than being in constant training for your marathon.

Just Do It

Start practicing today. As you walk around and do your ordinary daily tasks, take note of your experiences. When you forget to describe things, don't berate yourself—just gently bring your mind back on track and remember to do it next time. There's no trick to it; just start describing to yourself the things you experience.

When you do this regularly, you're making new connections in your brain. Then, next time you're writing something—any-thing—and you need a good description for "musty," your brain will retrieve that "old camp bag" that you mentally recorded while you were trying to define the smell you had in your base-ment before you took to it with a blowtorch.

Think of it as stocking your cabinets. Every time you define something with your writer's perceptions, you're adding another can of soup to the pantry. Next time you're feeling a little under the weather, you've got that soup to just pull out and heat up.

Stock those cabinets with great definitions for characters, emotions, and experiences. It will make your writing much easier when you can simply draw upon your memories rather than starting from scratch each time, trying to crank out brand new words and phrases that your brain has never processed before. You know how it's always easier to come up with a cliché, like "old as dirt" or "soft as a baby's bottom?" It's your job to stick old and soft into the food processor in your brain and spin them around and around until you've turned them into something new—old as your boyfriend's socks, or soft as rising bread dough.

Respect Your Language

To be a writer, you must have a profound respect for language. Language is how we communicate, and a writer must be an ef-fective communicator. Knowing proper spelling and grammar won't make you a writer, but you're handicapping yourself un-necessarily if you don't take the time to learn the basics.

Today I got an e-mail with this subject line: "Artical for Absolute Write." I didn't even need to open the e-mail to know this was not someone I'd want writing for me.

The rules of grammar exist for a very good reason: they help us all understand how to interpret the words on a page. Misplaced or missing commas can change the whole meaning of a sentence. "Let's eat, Harry" is a lot different than "Let's eat Harry." Improperly used semicolons can slow down a read and make it laborious instead of enjoyable. Think of improper grammar as a clogged shower drain. You want your water to run through the pipes freely; you don't want hairballs and soap bits to hinder the flow.

Likewise, you don't want your insecurities about usage to slow down your writing. Think of how much more smoothly you could write if you didn't have to stop to ask yourself whether a period goes inside or outside the quotation marks (the answer is "inside," by the way).

In his book *Make Your Words Work*, Gary Provost writes, "If you constantly make those major grammatical mistakes, you have not developed a true ear for the language, and chances are you are also not properly tuned into the subtleties and connotations of words, the rhythm of sentences or the sour note in a sentence or paragraph, and you are a lot further (or is it farther?) from being a good writer than you thought. You must go back and take a course in grammar, but this time learn it with your ears, not with your eyes."

If you're insecure about your grammatical skills, I highly suggest that you take some time to study your language. Take a night course in English composition, or at the very least, pick up a book or two on the subject and engage in some serious self-paced studying. *The Elements of Style* by William Strunk, Jr. and E. B. White is a popular guide, and at only 105 pages, it won't weigh you down. Barbara Wallraff's *Word Court* is another good choice; it'll keep you entertained while you're learning.

▶ PROMPT: Write about loss.

The Beauty of Being a Newbie

You don't need a permit to become a writer. While a master's degree in creative writing from Harvard just might help, there have been plenty of best-selling authors who never went to college or even finished high school. There are myriad ways to learn the craft of writing—and the most important way for you to learn is to read, read, read, and then write, write, write.

When you're new to writing, not only is your page a blank canvas, but *you* are a blank canvas. Your writing can take any direction, and can teach you things about the world and about yourself that you might never have learned otherwise. Allow yourself to be open to all possibilities, and remind yourself that you don't have to be perfect. Your sole job is to get words down on paper. You can deal with making those words right later, but for now, just slap on that first coat of paint. So what if it's streaky or the wrong color? You're just putting down the foundation. There's plenty of time to be perfect later.

I switched from writing nonfiction to fiction about four years ago. One problem I confronted was that I couldn't describe things very well—gardens where I didn't know the names of various flowers, living rooms where I wanted something more luxurious than what sat in my own. I began to scan old magazines from garage sales and cut out things that appealed to my eye, saving them in plastic sheets and storing them in a three-ring binder. Where possible, I kept the description from the article. The binder is now three inches thick.

When we moved into our condo last year, I couldn't write. There was so much negative energy here. I was totally blocked. Then a friend visited, and as we were having coffee, her eye caught the binder. She said she had never seen anyone but a lawyer use a binder that thick, and wanted to know what was in it. I explained. That night, I pulled out the binder and found a picture of a magnificent English garden. I started to describe it in my own words, and as I was writing, thoughts in a jumble started—story ideas, plots, characters.

Thanks to an English garden, I am now at work on my second novel, The Nefarious Lawyer.

—Cheryl Ryshpan, writer

3

Myths from the Meanies

Some rules are important. (As in, "Don't smoke while you're pregnant.") Others aren't. (Like that label on your mattress that says, "Do Not Remove Under Penalty of Death.") And still others are opinions parading as rules. (Such as "Lather. Rinse. Repeat.")

With writing, craft rules say things like, "screenplays must adhere to a three-act structure" and "your protagonist must have a character arc" and "don't use passive voice." Should you know these rules? Of course you should. And they may prove very helpful. They may also stand in your way. It's up to you to decide whether or not to break these types of rules; if you do so, do it on purpose and for good reason.

Now that that's out of the way, let me tell you what I think of the rest of the "rules," the ones that deal with the *how* and *why* of writing: they're a bunch of hooey.

Hooey, I say. And here's why: in a subject like math, you need rules. If one plus one *didn't* equal two, although tax time would be a lot more fun, the folks at educational book publisher McGraw-Hill would be in real trouble. Subjects like science, physics, and geometry need rules, too. Little Jimmy who keeps putting gum in Suzy's hair needs rules. Prisons need plenty of rules.

But writers? We don't need a lot of stinkin' rules. We're the ones who are supposed to *break* the rules, remember? Writing is a world of fantasy and imagination, creativity and thought. Even if you're a technical writer, you're still faced with the same blank page each day, and it's your job to fill it. But like a pinball ricocheting through a dozen blinking lights and flashing bumpers, a writer's job is to navigate through those rules and be as creative as possible.

And yet writers come up against just as many rules as the working mathematician, scientist, or doctor.

Unfortunately, teachers and editors are only two thirds of the battle. The final third rests in your fellow writers themselves. As pained as I am to say it, writers, especially those who have had a (very) small taste of success, are often the worst offenders of all, liberally tossing around the various rules that place as many shackles, chains, and limits on a writer as does writer's block itself.

They're the ones who tell you that your novel must be 80,000 words and that your screenplay won't sell unless it's high concept and has an A-list actor attached. They're the ones who spout off about which genres are "dead" and which ones are "hot." They have opinions coming out their dust jackets, and their small taste of success has given them the false notion that they are now world authorities on writing.

Maybe the writers who foist these so-called rules upon other writers are well intentioned. Maybe they truly believe that their way is the only way. Or maybe they're evil people who want to make you feel inferior. Either way, they're plain wrong. Allow me to elaborate on some of these myths masquerading as rules.

1. **"You must write every day."** Nonsense. Okay, if your job depends on it, sure. But otherwise, don't you dare feel

bad if your natural writing rhythm is to work in spurts, or just to write on weekends, or every second Tuesday, or whenever your mother-in-law comes to visit.

When I write a screenplay, I do so quickly and furiously. I let the idea percolate for a few weeks, and then when I sit down to do the actual writing, it comes out in a grand spastic fit. My hygiene and eating habits suffer; I work around the clock for days on end and completely forget about doing human things like brushing my hair and changing out of pajamas. (If you hate your friends, this is a great way to make sure none of them pop over to visit.) My fish flips through the phone book to find the number for animal protection groups that will come over and make me change the sludge water in his tank, and my fiancé wanders by menacingly every now and then, threatening to unplug my computer if I don't come-here-right-this-minute-and-eat-the-meal-he-has-so-lovingly-cooked-for-me.

I write like this, not letting the outside world in, until I've typed "Fade Out" and done the same. Then I may not write another script for months, or even a year.

However, my "real job" is writing, too—not screenplays, but articles and books. I do write every day, but not necessarily creatively. Writing every day keeps me in shape and in practice for the writing I love. But I know plenty of writers who don't write every day and still manage to write gorgeous prose when they do set pen to paper.

It's easy to get blocked when you're busy beating yourself up over the idea that you don't write often enough. "It's just self-imposed guilt, I think. Performance anxiety," says screenwriter Jeff O'Brien. "I mean, if you just want to go to sleep beside your wife after a long day, you don't say you have lover's block." And he's right. That's called "being married."

Mastery is mostly made up of habit. If you want your writing to be as good as it can be, then write as often as you can. Write in the nooks and crannies of life, while dinner is on the stove or during your lunch hour. Write on trains and in the bathroom (does anyone know where to get lined toilet paper?). Write instead of watching television. Wake up an hour early and write before anyone else gets up. Write as often as you want to write.

Keeping a writing schedule helps many writers. It's kind of like exercise; when you're out of shape, those first few days of aerobic exercise can be as enjoyable as a trip to the proctologist. However, the more you do it, the easier it gets, and the more benefit you reap from it. (The writing, that is. I'm not recommending weekly visits to your proctologist.) You may go to the gym every Monday, Wednesday, and Friday at 5:00 P.M. Allocating a specific time for working out helps you to stay motivated, and after a while, it just becomes routine; your body expects a good workout on those days.

Likewise, if you decide you're going to write every Tuesday, Friday, and Saturday at 8:00 A.M., you may find that you don't quite know what to do with yourself those first few sessions, but you're slowly programming your brain to recognize writing time and react to it accordingly. Be patient with yourself and just decide to have fun during your scheduled time, no matter what the output looks like. Be willing to act spontaneously and surprise yourself. Maybe all you'll come up with is a hideous haiku, and maybe you'll crank out an editorial about why "This Little Piggy Went to Market" is offensive to our porcine friends—he wasn't going to the market to do his shopping, you know!

If you can get rid of your block and rediscover all the reasons you want to write in the first place, then no one should have to tell you to write regularly because you won't be able to drag yourself away from it. You'll loathe interruptions instead of hoping for them.

2. **"You must isolate yourself to write."** Bulldinkle. Some people work best in the same manner as I do when I'm working on a screenplay, and others prefer writing in the middle of cafés and libraries.

But more important, a harmful myth exists that writers are supposed to be solitary creatures in general, living in the mountains and abhorring human contact. Tell me this: without rich life experiences, what would you write about? What would your words be worth if they didn't come from a place of deep human understanding? You only get that understanding by throwing yourself out there in the world and meeting people, listening to conversations, observing seasons changing, traveling, visiting friends of different ethnic backgrounds, and testing your horizons.

So, be social. Say "yes" to engagements. Join groups. Find ways to meet people you wouldn't ordinarily meet. (Make sure your insurance is paid up if you're planning to bump them from behind in your car). And forget that "writer-as-hermit" cliché.

3. **"You must outline before you write."** Eek, just writing that makes me hear my high school English teacher's voice, demanding that I turn in my outline before I start the "real" writing. She actually graded our outlines.

Boo, hiss. Some people work best with outlines, and others don't. I outline my nonfiction books and some long articles, but doing so with fiction distills the joy right out of the actual writing process for me.

Part of the reason I write is because *I* want to know what happens next! When I'm forced to think the whole thing through and know exactly where everything is headed, I lose all motivation to write the darn thing. The mystery is gone. I write to solve the mystery for myself, above everyone else. I may have these great characters all worked out in my mind, but I don't know if they're going to turn left or right at that corner when they come to it, or whether they'll go straight ahead and get hit by a bus. I don't want to know. I want them to tell me when we get to it.

My characters keep me up at night. They make unreasonable demands—ordering me to get out of my cozy bed and back to the computer so they can have adventures. When I formally outline, they quit doing that. What a loss.

There is no one correct way of outlining or of preparing to write. I know lots of people who use index cards, writing each scene on a card. Others take pages of notes and store them in folders. Others write completely by the seat of their pants, though I advise at least a pen and paper.

What works for you is what's right for you. And that's all there is to it. If you normally write without an outline and now you're blocked, try writing an outline. It *can* help quite a bit—it's much harder to get blocked if you have a solid map of where your story is headed. If you normally outline, toss it and write whatever comes to you.

4. **"You must write three (or five, or ten) pages a day."** Just like the "you-must-write-every-day" rule, the rules that dictate how much you must complete are just advice worded too strongly. It's great to set goals, but every writer has a different threshold for output. Write until you have to quit, or until your partner switches off the

power. And then don't feel guilty—just put it down and promise yourself you'll pick it up again as soon as you possibly can. Disclaimer: this does not apply if you have a deadline, so don't you dare tell your editor, "But Jenna said I should quit without feeling guilty!" Nay, you get that bottom in the chair and write until your fingers hurt, and then you write some more, until you are Done. (Did I hear a whip cracking?)

5. **"Real writers don't write for free."** Oh yeah? I've written for national magazines, books, and major anthologies, and I still write for free sometimes. Not very often, but sometimes. I do it when I particularly want to support a publication that can't afford to pay, or when I'll get valuable publicity from my efforts.

   Many experienced writers complain when new writers work for free or accept unfavorable contract terms; their thinking is that this devalues the entire industry and lets publishers believe they can get writers without paying a fair wage. While there is logic in this thinking, it's too black and white and doesn't take into account how a writer with no credits can break into the industry. Oftentimes, beginning writers happily accept assignments from publications that can't afford to pay—and in return, the writer gets a clip and the first taste of exposure.

   So, if you're just starting out and are wondering whether or not to offer your work to nonpaying markets, listen to both sides of the argument from writers who are further along in their careers. Think hard about all of the pros and cons. And then make your decision based on your own ethics, not anyone else's rule.

6. **"You can't start writing without a title."** This is perhaps one of the most odious—not to mention erroneous— "rules" of

them all. I was sitting in the movie theater the other day—
one of the perks of being a freelance writer—and was just a
few minutes early. Before the previews started, humongous
slides flashed across that big old movie screen, most likely
to keep the impatient teens in the audience from ripping
apart the seat cushions and setting the popcorn tubs on
fire out of sheer boredom. Some slides were movie trivia,
some were celebrity quotes, some were pictures of fizzing
sodas and ketchup-slathered hot dogs designed to send us
all back to the concession stand by sending subliminal messages: "Buy a large popcorn, or you'll develop a pronounced limp and an embarrassing speech impediment."

However, two or three were called "Fizzled Movie Titles." These told you the working titles to some of your favorite films before they settled on the blockbuster title
you ask for down at the video store. For instance, did you
know that the working title for the movie *Unbreakable,*
starring Samuel L. Jackson and Bruce Willis, was actually
No Ordinary Hero? Nope? Me neither.

And now that you know, does it change your perspective about the film? Probably not. Would one of its heavy-
hitting stars have bowed out if the studio had stuck with
the original title? Doubt it. Would the film itself, the plot,
the camera angles, the special effects, have been any less
effective if the title had had three words in it instead of
just one? Hardly.

The point is, what if M. Night Shyamalan had simply
sat around, twiddling his thumbs and killing precious
time while he waited for *Unbreakable* to pop into his
crowded head? Nothing. Absolutely nothing. His script
might never have been written, and his movie might
never have been made.

As with scripts, so goes it with all other types of writing. Often, the very best titles come to you while you're actually in the process of writing. Maybe it's the name of a favorite character that pops up midway through your novel. Maybe it's a catch phrase used by your dastardly villain. Maybe it's a play on words you stumble across in your final edits—or that pops into your head at 3 A.M. on the very morning you're due to send your manuscript to the publisher. Maybe it's what you yelled when you stubbed your toe on the corner of the desk. Whatever your title, don't be afraid not only to start writing without one, but to change it halfway through, or even when it's all done.

And don't get too attached to it anyway. Titles are one of the things over which a writer has the least control. I had this terrific book I originally called *Slaying the Dragon*. When the publisher told me it wasn't clear what the book was about (anxiety disorders), I suggested *Slaying the Anxiety Dragon*. Then the editor gave me a list of about ten possible titles that the marketing team had devised. I picked two or three that I liked. They gleefully ignored me and named the book *Conquering Panic and Anxiety Disorders*, one of the most boring titles ever to exist on any planet.

Skip the title. Just write the darn thing.

7. **"Pick a genre and stick to it."** This old rule has been following writers around since the beginning of time—or historical romances, take your pick. If everyone bought into this, nonfiction writers would never write fiction, and vice versa. No romance writer could ever cross over into mainstream thrillers. (Sorry, Linda Howard.) No horror writer could ever write books for kids. (Sorry, Dean Koontz.) No

children's writer could ever write a true crime book. (Sorry, Lois Duncan.) And no politician could ever write his autobiography. (Okay, maybe it's valid in some cases.)

Naturally, some writers fall into certain categories and it's hard to see them any other way, especially if they've hit it big and gone on to top the best-seller lists in a way that's as public as it is profitable. But while it's hard to picture Sebastian Junger writing the next *Bridget Jones's Diary* or Helen Fielding writing the next *Perfect Storm*, who's to say it couldn't happen, or shouldn't happen?

After all, even though people refer to Stephen King as the "king of horror," who can deny the versatility of such human dramas as *Stand by Me* and *The Shawshank Redemption*? And if Ann Rule had stuck to writing only for those true detective magazines, who could have ever written such true crime classics as *The Stranger Beside Me* and *Small Sacrifices*?

If you've got writer's block, this is the biggest rule for you to avoid, bar none. Crossing over into another genre may just be your ticket out of writer's block purgatory and straight into writing utopia. If your novel's not working out, why not condense it into a kids' book? And if your science fiction story about giant radioactive earwigs falls flat, send it to *National Enquirer*—they'll probably put it on the front page.

Switch-hitting from one writing genre to the next could just mean swinging through another strikeout to writing a home run.

8. **"You must write about what you know."** Hogwash. Writing about what you know is a great jumping-off point. But people get caught up in thinking that everything they write has to be autobiographical, or has to be about

characters who reflect their exact life experiences (i.e., a middle-class Caucasian woman can only write about middle-class Caucasian women characters). What's your story really about? Maybe it's about betrayal. You know how it feels to be betrayed. Being betrayed doesn't feel any different if you're Latino, male, and rich. It just means you can afford a better shrink.

Write about emotions you know, but not necessarily plots you've lived. Do you know what it's like to have a miscarriage? Maybe not, but I'm quite certain you know the feeling of loss. I trust that you can take your experience with loss and translate it to your character's feelings about her miscarriage. Trust yourself to know how to empathize; trust that you can put yourself in your fictitious characters' shoes and write believably about them.

I write to learn and expand my horizons. It would be terribly limiting and boring if I chose only to write about things I already know. Rather, I make it a point to write about things I *want* to know instead.

I wanted to learn more about disabilities issues, so I began pitching articles about how people with Down syndrome can't get heart transplants, and about government antidiscrimination policies. I didn't know a whole lot about these things before I began querying; I chose to learn about them, and then write about them.

To be a great writer, be a great researcher. If you want to write a coming-of-age story about a young Baptist woman who rebels against her strict upbringing, then visit Baptist churches. Listen in on girls' conversations. Introduce yourself, ask questions, and soak in all the details. Not only will this help the story you're working on initially, but it just may lead to your next story.

After observing some rowdy high school kids at a local mall once, I decided to write an article on "those darn kids today." Sitting in on an in-school suspension program at a local high school provided me with reams of material, some of which made it into a reader's column for a local newspaper. The head of the local juvenile detention center read it thoroughly, found my phone number through the newspaper, and eventually invited me to rewrite a 300-page manual used with "problem kids" to build self-esteem.

You never know where your research will lead. And that's the fun part.

At the root of good writing is honesty; your writing must be so real that readers will take your hand and follow you through every meandering trail. They must trust your voice. The only way to achieve this is to tell them the truth about your characters' lives.

"But . . . I made up my characters," you say? I may be mentally ill, but I'm not crazy. Of course you made them up. But they must be real, three-dimensional, deep characters with hopes, dreams, fears, regrets, flaws, and passions. You must know them as well as you know your best friends and you must transfer that knowledge to your readers, so they can cross that line between fantasy and reality and become engulfed in your story. "Remember it's easy for the reader to close the book on a two-dimensional character," says novelist Woody Wilson.

Don't fake it. Faking it is showing up to interview someone before you've read about his background. Faking it is praying your stupid questions will elicit brilliant answers. You must ask brilliant questions if you expect brilliant answers, unless you're talking to a politician, in which case you're lucky if you get any answers at all. The same rule applies to fiction. Talk to your characters; spend lots of time with pre-interviews. That's right—I want you to literally ask your characters questions. Learn everything there is to know about your characters.

You may find out that you've hired a smoker to be a soccer player, or that you hired a man who's afraid of heights to be a roofer. Make sure your character is qualified for the job you're giving him—but don't let his life run too smoothly. There's nothing interesting about a girl who grows up wanting to be a teacher, then becomes a teacher and has a successful career. Ho hum. There's something interesting about a girl who grows up wanting to be a teacher, almost does, but winds up being a garbage collector instead. Why? I don't know—you tell me.

▶ PROMPT: What is your character's biggest regret?

9. **"A true writer takes months or years to write a book."** For some dumb reason, both the general public and some fellow writers are particularly suspicious of any piece of work that has been produced quickly. It's quite possible that your block is trying to appease this wrongful perception. After all, we've all heard stories about the masters who spent ten years just toiling away on one novel. We second-guess ourselves when our pages are flying faster than our printers can spit them out. We don't know whether to brag or lie when we whip out a finished manuscript in just a matter of weeks. Certainly, we wouldn't

want our readers to find out; they might see our work as less valuable.

Lawrence Block discusses this phenomenon in his book *Telling Lies for Fun and Profit*, speculating that people may find it galling to pay for a book that seems to have come too easily to its author. "The stuff's supposed to read as though it came naturally and effortlessly, but one wants to be assured that a soul-satisfying amount of hard work went into it. Well, the public be damned. The same public goes to prize fights to see boxers flattened and attends auto races hoping desperately to witness a crash."

Not only does each author have a different natural pace, but that pace can significantly change from one piece to the next. Every now and then, a manuscript may emerge fully hatched in record time with absolutely no need for rewriting. And other times, it'll be slow going and require numerous drafts. Neither way cheapens the writing, and neither guarantees a higher level of quality.

Who Makes Up These Rules?

Though unions and writing groups abound, there is no one governing body for writers. We simply pick up a pen and pad of paper, plug in our typewriter, or boot up our computer—and start writing.

Only you can make up your own set of writing rules. Only you can decide when you title your book or how many pages you write a day or which genre you write in or where you write or what you write. Should you follow the specific guidelines for each magazine or publisher you write for? Absolutely. But should some snooty-toot novelist be able to tell you what time to start writing in the morning? Never. Some of you probably don't even recognize mornings anymore. (Hint: the sun is in the east.)

Making Your Own Rules

Where to Start

And who ever said you had to start at the beginning? Start on page 2. Start on page 82. I started this book somewhere in the middle, and jumped all around. I wrote this paragraph after I'd already written chapter 16.

If you can't figure out where to start, but you have a strong idea of your ending, then write the ending first. If you've already started, but you've hit a block, then skip that part and write the rest. You can always write in the missing pieces later.

You can even just write random scenes and figure out where they may fit at another time. If you're just stuck on one part, don't let that stop you from writing all around it. The great thing about your audience is that they'll never know the difference. You are the writer. The captain of your own ship, the engineer of your own caboose. Only you know where the next stop is, or if you should go back and pick up somebody you forgot to get along the way, or even drop off somebody you don't like anymore. Change the plans. Switch things. Interrupt. No one will ever know.

Ever watched one of today's modern DVDs "packed with never-before-seen footage?" Why was it never seen before? Because the director, the studio, or even some big name actor wanted it cut, gone, kaput. Did it matter the first time you watched the movie? Obviously not. How could you have known there was another hour and a half of outtakes, alternate endings, misleading plot twists, bad lighting, and behind-the-scenes footage lying on the cutting room floor? The fact is, you didn't. And neither will your audience.

Don't Should On Yourself

No matter what you write or how you write it, be sure you're writing what you want to write and not what you think you *should* write. If you're not having fun writing it, no one will have fun reading it.

I've seen it happen to too many writers; they may love reading romance novels, but they believe that's not high enough literary art, so they force themselves to write outside of their preferred genre. You might just be a terrific romance novelist. It's not important what anyone else thinks of you—it's important what *you* think of you. If you think you could have a grand old time writing romance, then do it.

Where to Get Ideas

Another myth is that great ideas are supposed to just come to writers. Like we're all just walking around, minding our own business, when *wham!* A great idea falls out of the heavens and lands in our brains (*now* I know what causes those headaches!). I know lots of writers who are blessed with this kind of talent. My good friend Sable Jak is an idea factory. She, and others, have so many ideas they'll never have enough years to use them all.

I, on the other hand, am idea-challenged. The idea fairy rarely visits my home without my asking. I have to invite her, cajole her, and then sometimes bang her over the head with a stick and drag her unconscious body into my abode without my neighbors calling the police. My muse is my mortgage.

So, if you're one of those writers with a lifetime full of ideas, consider yourself blessed and my hero. If not, I regard myself as pretty good company. Don't beat yourself up because you need help in coming up with ideas. I use a variety of sources to find new ideas. These include:

- Writing prompts, like the ones you see throughout this book
- Song lyrics (Country songs are particularly helpful, because they often tell a whole story.)
- Newspaper and magazine articles (Read your local paper and see if you can find a story that deserves a wider audience—or do the reverse; read a major newspaper or magazine and see if you can find a local angle to write about in your town paper.)
- The Internet (Looking for ideas for health articles? Visit health Web sites. Looking for humorous inspiration? Visit humor sites.)
- Strangers' conversations (Most writers are great eavesdroppers. Listen in on conversations on the train and at the coffee shop, then go home and use the dialogue in a story, or make up the speakers' life stories.)
- Other writers (In one of my writing groups, we regularly "donate" ideas to other writers—we figure that if one of us isn't going to follow up on an idea he had, he can pass it along to someone who might need a fresh idea.)

▶ PROMPT: Pick up a magazine and look at the advertisements. Many of the pictures will be provocative and ripe for storytelling. Come up with new captions, or write a story about the characters you see.

Pave Your Own Path

Each writer paves his or her own road to success, and the methods behind our madness are wildly varied. Find out what works for you and don't apologize for it. Write your own rule book, and if it stops working, violate those rules and write new ones. Keep evolving and learning as a writer and concern yourself only with filling your own shoes. Whether you accomplish that by writing ten pages a day first thing in the morning in the basement or by jotting down poems in code while hanging upside down from your favorite tree branch every third Tuesday, remember that your uniqueness is the most cherished gift in your writer's savings account.

4

Planning, Scheming, and Dreaming

Determine Your Motivation

I thought I was writing *A Girl I Almost Knew*, a mostly autobiographical screenplay, so I could pay off my obscene mortgage. Screenwriters make scads of money. Oodles. Silly amounts. When they sell, of course. Which is about as likely a prospect as teaching a muskrat to belch the alphabet. But you can never tell that to an aspiring screenwriter, me included. Damn the torpedoes, full speed ahead. Look out William Goldman.

So, there I was, pouring my guts into this script, telling myself that I was uncovering these painful memories about my past so I could exploit them and make them earn their keep. My traumatic childhood had to be good for something, I reasoned. It would be the grist for a character-driven script that would be so compelling that a producer would weep and throw buckets of money at me. And I would soon be doing lunch with Stevie Spielberg, and he'd hire me to write *ET2*.

It was a hard script to write. When someone came into the room, I'd scroll down quickly so no one could read what I was writing. My heart raced as I wrote emotional scenes. I wrote the truth, ugly and raw. And when I was done, I posted it on American Zoetrope's Web site (www.zoetrope.com) for feedback from other writers.

I was used to checking for new reviews every 8.3 seconds with prior scripts, but this time I was a raw nerve ending, sweating and palpitating, dying in a vat of my own desperation.

Please, let them like it. I don't care about the reviews; I'm a consummate professional. *I'll flat out die if they hate it.* No, I want them to rip it apart. How else will I know what needs improvement? *For the love of Zeus, let them tell me it's brilliant.*

It was a hard script to read. Even the people who didn't know me surmised that it was autobiographical. Every time a new review came in, my ears got hot and throbbed. I could barely stand to read them; what if they said my story was stupid? I wasn't just looking for validation as a writer. I was looking for validation as a person. That's a pretty tall order.

Most of the reviews were kind, probably too kind because everyone sensed that I might just be sitting at the other end of the computer with a loaded gun pointed at my forehead.

For a few weeks, my entire world teetered on the edge of those reviews. A good one meant that I had landed on a base and the umpire announced I was safe. A bad one meant I was a pus-laden sore infecting humanity by my very presence.

And as time went on, I came to realize that I had been lying to myself. I didn't write that script for money. I wrote it as therapy. And I had no business showing this diary to strangers; it was far too volatile a situation.

I had determined that writing for catharsis wasn't a worthwhile goal. I was a professional writer, after all, and by definition that meant that I was supposed to make money from my writing. I wasn't supposed to be so self-indulgent that I would write something just for myself.

But writing can serve many functions and a writer's goals can change with every piece, every day. I stopped trying to market that particular script and instead, put it aside like an old diary that I will undoubtedly visit again someday. It has already served its primary function—it helped me purge some very difficult emotions and express parts of myself that I had kept locked away. In the end, that mattered more than the reviews.

Your Reasons Are the Right Reasons

Be honest with yourself about your motivations for writing and reassess them often. You're allowed to write for whatever reason strikes you. If you need to write something, write it. Don't worry about whether it's salable.

And, in a surprising number of cases, it's exactly when you quit trying to be a mind reader about what is commercial or what's hot in today's publishing climate and you just write from your gut that you come up with something that will actually resonate with people and *will* sell.

Of course, the reality can seem mighty different. We all know the genres that are flying off the shelf this month, the summer beach books that flood Borders every May and June, or the cookie-cutter gift books that litter the shelves from October to January. We know the subjects that are sizzling hot and those that are stone-cold dead. We know the popular authors and, most of the time, what their books will sound like before we even open page 1. And there's nothing wrong with that.

But never ever *ever* forget the quirky little books that pound the competition, defy the native genres, and perhaps even start new genres of their own. Those books are not born of formulas or templates, and to read them is like tapping into the author's obscene joy for his subject matter and sheer thrill of capturing lightning in a bottle.

▶ PROMPT: Write about a secret you accidentally didn't keep.

Cognitive Dissonance Causes Writer's Block

When your real goals are in conflict with the goals you've imposed on yourself, this can cause uneasiness and creative blocks. Psychologists call this "cognitive dissonance"—when one of your beliefs is in conflict with another one. On the surface, you may believe that you're writing only for money. Deep down, your goal may be to change the world through your writing. Or you may think you're writing to share a story with the world when your real goal is to be changed by the experience of writing or to prove to yourself that you're a good writer. Cognitive dissonance causes tension, and tension just makes writer's block worse. The block may know full well what your true intentions are, even if you don't. It may be stomping its feet and crossing its arms in an attempt to bring you back to your honest goals. Turn on your ears and listen to what your block is telling you.

What can you learn from your block to help you not only overcome it right now, but avoid it the next time it comes knocking? What can your block tell you? What part of your writing psyche can it illuminate to show you what you've never seen before?

Writer's block can be a good thing when it shakes up your writing routine. It can make you look at your career, your goals, your current project, your whole identity from an entirely different perspective. It can show you that you're not done growing yet, not by a long shot.

Writer's block can say to you, "Look, pal. I know you think you know it all, but, guess what? You don't. Writing is a long and winding road to enjoy, not a destination to rush toward. You've come so far, but now you're at a crossroad and it's up to you to decide which way to go. Toward knowledge and enlightenment, or to stay on this path and keep yourself blocked up nice and tight. I've got things to show you, if you'll let me. And, oh, the places you'll go."

Some writers find themselves in a different situation. They tell themselves they're just writing for themselves, when they really harbor secret desires to be published. This is a means of self-preservation; by pretending they don't care about publication, they're saving themselves from rejection. After all, your work can't be rejected if you never send it out (unless your dog chews up your manuscript and then regurgitates it).

Do you really want to write or do you just want to have a finished product to show off? Many new writers need to admit to themselves that they have no desire to put in the hours, months, and years that it takes to master their craft; they just want to see their byline in print. They talk about the novels they'll never actually write—those blockbuster ideas that they're sure would make millions if only they could find the time to write. Eventually they'll take up fishing so they can bore people senseless about "the one that got away."

Making Time

Of course, there's no such thing as finding time—only *making* time. No extra hours are going to appear in your day just because you've decided to write. It's all a matter of prioritizing. If you make writing important in your life, you can make ways to let it happen. Because we're not all hedonists, we don't always do the things that bring us pleasure. No, we do the things we think we're supposed to, and we tell ourselves that enjoyment is frivolous and unnecessary. So, doing the dishes gets to the front of the line, and writing a short story gets put into the "maybe-another-day" pile. (Of course, if you're doing the dishes first because you *enjoy* doing them, then I've got a pile in my kitchen sink you're more than welcome to.)

The truth is that the dishes can wait. My dishes have been known to wait until the cows come home and hell freezes over. They're very patient, those dishes. You just write, and those dishes will sit there very quietly, barely moving at all, behaving extraordinarily well while you take care of the business of creativity.

Long-Term Goals

When you set long-term writing goals, be as specific as you can be. Be both realistic and pie-in-the-sky.

Your list might include:

- Finish writing mystery novel.
- Get an Association of Authors' Representatives (AAR)- member literary agent who specializes in mysteries.
- Break into the national women's magazine market.

Add to your list as often as the urge strikes and cross out goals that no longer suit you. Make sure the items on your list are what you really want and not what you think you should want. Keep your list somewhere nearby, where you can view it regularly.

Just the act of consciously writing down your goals can help you organize your priorities and set a game plan for achieving the things you most want to achieve. You can also reward yourself for checking off completed goals. You might buy yourself a new printer after selling an article to *Family Circle*, or a lap dance after landing a literary agent. If you're single. And into that sort of thing. And your new agent's not the one dancing for you. Ahem.

Change Is Good

Don't be afraid to try new things, and never be afraid to *write* new things. Think of writing the same way as you think of fashion. Would you still wear the same kinds of things you wore in high school? College? Well, then, why are you still writing the same kinds of things you wrote when you were in high school or college?

Sure, we all know those jeans-and-T-shirt people who have always looked the same and dressed the same. Similarly, many writers know what they want from a very young age, and write and write and write until they finally get there. But as writers, we evolve on a daily basis whether we realize it or not.

Don't be afraid to write a Clancy-esque techno-thriller, even if all you've ever written is Bombeck-esque personal essays. Look on your bookshelves. Look in your entertainment center. If all the books you read are murder mysteries, if all of your videos feature the words "death," "murder," and "whodunit," yet you're a dogmatic Christian fiction writer—who's never finished a book—perhaps it's time for you to branch out and try something new.

Perhaps you're not experiencing writer's block. Perhaps you're really at a *road*block instead.

If you knew you'd never be published or paid, would you write anyway? What would you write for only the reward of writing? There's your long-term goal.

Like me, you may write other things to pay the bills—but even the bread-and-butter writing should be enjoyable. I am an odd creature in that I actually enjoy writing press releases, and I enjoy researching for science and health-related articles. They don't give me the same abounding joy I experienced as a child while eating that fizzy rock candy that pops on your tongue, but it's a quieter sort of joy.

If you're writing full-time (or aim to), don't pigeonhole yourself into areas that you think are lucrative, but not enjoyable. You might as well stick to a 9-to-5er with a boss who sucks out your will to live if you're going to dread writing. At least he pays you while he sucks.

Rather, plan for success *and* joy at the same time. Am I starting to sound like a motivational speaker? I'm going to cut that out right now.

▶ PROMPT: Write about the first time you can remember feeling humiliated.

Set Your Weekly Objectives

Lots of people talk about setting goals. I'm not unique in suggesting that you do so. But what I'm suggesting is that you take it a step further and plot out just how you will achieve your goals—I want you to keep a running list of weekly objectives.

It's simple to write, "I want to be a best-selling children's author." But how does that help you to get there?

That's why your weekly objectives should include the steps you'll take to achieve your larger goals. Having a fully conceived game plan can help you stave off writer's block by keeping you on track. So what kinds of steps belong on your weekly objectives?

If you're going to write children's stories, first, you'll want to read what's out there in the market now. Children's books today look a whole lot different than they did when you were a kid. You might allot a whole month just to reading. Write down titles of books you want to read, or names of authors who are gaining recognition. You'll also want to read books or take courses about children's writing. Your weekly objective might be to research on-line courses, or to sign up for a children's writing class at a community college. Then you may want to read publishers' guidelines in a book like the *Writer's Market.*

Next comes the brainstorming. Your written goal may be to come up with three possible story lines. Then you'll choose one and come up with a title and character names. Your next objective is to write a short outline (if that helps you), or a short summary of what you intend to write.

You may want to check out similar works for inspiration and direction. Writer Shaun Fawcett suggests, "Get an actual sample of the type of document that you need to write. It could be something that you wrote previously, or it could be something from an old working file, a clipping from a magazine article, or a sales brochure you picked up." For example, when I was working on a media kit for Absolute Write, I studied lots of media kits to pick up ideas for formatting and content. Some writers are afraid to read similar works; they're worried that if they pick up ideas from other sources, they're "stealing" from the other writer. Unless you're just thinly rewording what the other author wrote, don't worry. It's perfectly all right to use other writers' works to light your fuse. Or, if it's particularly bad, your fireplace.

Now, you'll tackle the fun part: the writing. Start wherever you like and end before you run out of things to say. Do that as many times as is necessary until you have a draft to work with. If you're new to writing, estimate how much time you think it'll take for you to finish writing this piece. Then double it.

Finally, the editing and proofreading. Give yourself at least a day or two off on your schedule before beginning your editing time. You'll have a much fresher perspective if you haven't seen the material for a few days, and you'll be more comfortable with "killing your darlings."

I want you to make me a promise that you'll really write out your weekly objectives. They are not set in stone, and you may find that in the beginning your expectations are too lofty (no, you can't write that whole novel in two weeks). But they'll give you a way to stay on track and mark your progress.

Buy a day planner and write all of your weekly objectives at the beginning of the week. Give yourself one of those satisfying check marks or a sticker as you complete each task.

Think of it as a self-imposed homework schedule. In school, if your teacher never told you when your homework was due, would you ever have done it? Now you're your own teacher and you set the rules. Tell yourself what your homework is and when it's due. And no extensions without a note from your mother!

When someone has an injury, she often undergoes physical therapy afterward. Well, writer's block is your injury, and you're going to have to do some writing therapy—which entails setting goals and weekly objectives and proving to yourself that you can achieve them. You may have to go easy on yourself at the onset, but as you heal you'll show yourself that you can take on bigger and bigger projects.

Carving Out Writing Time Despite Family Obligations

"My writer's block is usually made up mostly of guilt," says novelist and produced screenwriter Genie Davis. "Guilt that I am not earning more money from my writing, supporting my family, paying attention to my family, paying attention to my business, et cetera. Once I get in that mode, I'm just stuck, frozen, inadequate—why bother? Either surprisingly or not, because I do believe that writing is my drug of choice and I am fairly heavily addicted to mainlining at least a thousand words a day, the best way to overcome this is to just talk myself out of my guilt. If I write for a couple of hours, then I'll pay the bills, make sales calls, do the laundry, or whatever it is that's hanging like a rusty axe over my head. I bargain with my own devils."

Most writers carry around a tremendous sense of guilt. We feel guilty because we want to hide out in our caves and write, at least until the bats drive us nuts. Because after all, if our writing isn't earning us big bucks, it's really just a glorified hobby. And hobbies are trivial; they're for selfish people or people with lots of free time.

We think we're supposed to do more cooking and PTAing. We scold ourselves for being so self-absorbed as to spend time writing when we could be spending quality time with our families. And our families waste no time in pointing this out, either. "Are you going to be done soon?" they ask. How could any of us get any writing done with all this guilt hanging over our heads?

You've got to claim some time for yourself. Recognize that every great piece of writing took time to write. Think of your absolute favorite books of all time—books that shaped your life. If those authors had felt so guilty about spending time alone that they decided to play the role of Suzy the Self-Sacrificing Homemaker, what would you advise them? "You must write!" you'd say. "Your writing is going to make a difference. People are going to enjoy and remember your work. Tell your family that."

Now advise yourself. Tell yourself that you can still be a great spouse, parent, worker, and friend even if you have this peculiar habit of needing to spend time alone on a regular basis.

When you're satisfied with your own life, you can be even better at all of your other roles. An unhappy person is rarely a good mate. Be in it for the long haul; know that if you spend time taking an honest shot at your writing career, you'll be more fulfilled and you'll have more to give. If you carve out time to spend on meeting your creative goals, you'll be more fully present when it's time to be there for other people. Otherwise, you're likely to be distracted, thinking about your unfulfilled goals and unrealized dreams—even if it's on a subconscious level.

It's easy to get discouraged, especially when you're blocked. Not only do you have the usual dosage of writer's guilt, but now you can't even write. Not only do big New York editors reject your work, but now your fingers are actually rejecting typing what you want to say.

But when discouragement—and the block—have you thinking of chucking it all, just consider the alternative: not writing at all. Where will *that* get you? Will never writing again ever get you closer to your hopes and dreams? Will padlocking your keyboard make you a happier, healthier person? Will donating this year's *Writer's Market* and tucking away that half-finished novel safely under your mattress really make you a better spouse or parent? Or will it just make an uncomfortable lump in the bed that will make it hard to sleep?

Better to muddle through it and do your best, day by day. Better to practice the exercises in this book, try new forms of therapy, and focus on the problem at hand—your nasty case of writer's block—and not the heavy writer's baggage you've been carrying around all these years.

▶ PROMPT: A man has tapped a woman's phone. Why?

Mommy or Daddy's Writing Time

If you're a family person, you may have to train your family to accept writing time just as much as you have to train yourself to write. If at all possible, come up with a schedule. Maybe 7 P.M. to 10 P.M. every night will be your writing time. Maybe you can only squeeze it in from 5 P.M. to 6 P.M. Whatever you decide, tell your family what your schedule is. There are many ways to remind your family when you will be writing, and therefore unavailable. You might try any of these:

- Keep a calendar or dry-erase board on the refrigerator, and pencil in your writing time in big letters.
- If you have an office in your home, find something to hang from the doorknob, such as a red scrunchie or a do-not-disturb doorknob hanger, to signify that you are inside and working.
- You know those signs that shopkeepers sometimes have on their front doors—"Be back at . . ." plus a clock face, so they can tell patrons what time they'll be back in the store? Get one of those, and adjust it to tell your family what time they're allowed to come a-knockin'.
- Writer Katy Terrega puts on headphones when she wants to signal it's working time. Oh, she's not actually listening to anything. But her family assumes she can't hear them, so they don't bug her.

If you have children, you must be loving but firm about your writing time. If they learn that they can barge in on Daddy during writing time and get him to look over their homework, listen to a story, break up an argument, or fix a broken toy, they won't learn to recognize your boundaries, and you'll wonder what happened to all of your writing time. Teach them which situations are legitimate emergencies—like when someone is hurt or sick—and which situations will have to wait until writing time is over.

You may find that you have to work your schedule around your family's needs as well; if you have young children, they may not have the patience to wait for three hours when they want to talk to Daddy. Maybe your writing time will have to be broken into two or three chunks a day, or maybe you can schedule a fifteen-minute break halfway through your writing time when your children are allowed to come in.

Treat this schedule just as you would if there was a boss looming over you. Show up and do your best work.

Because I work a normal full-time job as well as part-time freelance writing, I use those boring weekly staff meetings to come up with ideas for articles. Initially, I spent one meeting writing up about thirty topics for articles. My niche is careers and job hunting, and my specialty within that realm is military-to-civilian transitions.

At other staff meetings, I used those thirty topics to start writing up "bullets" (one or two line blurbs) about the major points I wanted to make in the article. I need peace and quiet when I'm actually writing, so I wait until later to actually write the articles, but by that time, I've "rehearsed" my writing in my brain so when I sit down at the computer, I'm already more than 50 percent done.

—Gale Kennedy, writer

5

Percolate

Off In the Distance

As a writer, you've likely mastered the "off-in-the-distance" look. My fiancé likes to wave his hand in front of my face and ask things like, "Are you still with us?" The answer, if I must be truthful, is usually "no." I'm off in another world—the world of my latest piece. Or fantasizing about a piece of Brad Pitt. Take your pick.

It's amazing how often we can look like we're doing absolutely nothing, or doing something deceptively simple like weeding the garden or knitting, when in truth, we're doing some of our hardest work of all. We're percolating.

Because it may look to the outside world like we're not doing anything, we may question ourselves—"Why am I not writing? Why am I wasting my time daydreaming like this?" Because great stories are born from daydreams, that's why.

When a car wash employee isn't working, it's pretty obvious—he's not washing a car. He doesn't have to spend lots of time thinking about how he's going to wash the car. He doesn't have to plan out his method of attack or consider how he'll connect with the car owner. So car wash employees may not understand how you can be working while you're staring off into space.

In fact, most noncreative types won't understand. And who cares? The key thing is that *you* have to understand. Staring off into the distance doesn't mean you're lazy. You have to believe that you're doing necessary work at those times, and that the time you spend taking flights of fancy to let your mind wander where it will is not frivolous.

In an on-line chat at FearOfWriting.com, novelist Douglas Clegg discussed what he does when the writing isn't flowing: "I stop writing it and I let it percolate in my brain for as long as it takes. I don't talk about it with anyone. I essentially allow creativity to block up in my head and get constipated, pardon the expression. And then, when I finally can't resist writing anymore, I sit back down and write."

Spend as much time as you can staring off into the distance. It will only help you later on when you're trying to piece together your story.

▶ PROMPT: Use this sentence somewhere in a short story: "Now that she was gone, I was finally free to tell the truth."

Keep a Dream Journal

I'm such a taskmaster that I even want you to think like a writer in your sleep.

Did you know that everyone has dreams, every time they reach the rapid eye movement (REM) stage of sleep? Usually multiple dreams. Of course, most of us don't remember all of our dreams; some of us don't remember any of our dreams.

You can change that. I'm living proof.

I used to remember a dream maybe once a month or so. Then someone suggested that I keep a dream journal. "That's silly," I thought. "I'll write in it only once a month." But he told me that just the act of purposely trying to remember a dream and making the recording of it the very first thought every morning would help me to open up chasms in my mind that I didn't think existed.

So I dutifully started a new notebook. I kept it under my bed, and every morning, the first thing I did after opening my eyes was to pick up that notebook and record anything I could remember.

In the beginning, I often wouldn't remember more than the way the dream made me feel. I couldn't remember what had taken place in the dream, but I did know that I woke up feeling agitated, so I wrote that down—"I had an agitating dream. I woke up feeling like I'd been arguing with someone, but I don't know who or why."

The amazing thing about keeping this dream journal was that my friend's prediction came true: after a few weeks of this, I could remember my dreams almost every day. Occasionally, I could even remember more than one dream per night. I got so good at it that I started remembering other people's dreams.

Just write down whatever snippets you can remember, even if they make no sense and even if you know you're leaving out parts. Again, this will help you to think like a writer.

Since dreams don't usually follow the rules of logic and rarely have a well-developed plot that includes a beginning, middle, and end, don't expect to find full stories worthy of publication in your dreams. However, you can pick up scenes, emotions, and descriptions for use in your "real" writing.

Another wondrous thing about recording your dreams is that you get to see patterns. I discovered that my dreams nearly always included water. I had no idea of that until I looked back on my dream journal after several months, purposely looking for repeated themes. And there it was: One night, I dreamed I was in a pet store and the fish tanks had broken and I had to swim through the store. Another night, I was swimming in the ocean and had to eat drowned seagulls to survive. Another night, a cult was trying to brainwash me to sacrifice my faceless baby into an Olympic-sized swimming pool. Yes, I know that I have issues.

I picked up a few interesting books about dream analysis (my favorite is *The Mystical Magical Marvelous World of Dreams* by Wilda Tanner) and discovered that water is the dream symbol that represents all emotions. Depending on what condition the water was in and what I was doing with the water, I could gauge whether the dream was positive or negative. In her book, Tanner says, "Calm, clear water usually represents your spiritual attunement, while murky or muddy water would indicate the invasion of ulterior motives, unclean thoughts, muddled emotions and feelings." She devotes a whole chapter to dreams about water. Green water, for example, means you have to clean your fish tank.

When you get used to putting your dreams into words, you can begin to understand them. And it's one more way that you can effortlessly break your writer's block: you don't need to come up with fresh ideas—your subconscious mind will supply them if you are receptive to them. You don't even have to make sure the plot is cohesive or the characters are fleshed out; your only job is to record exactly what you remember. Your brain makes up stories all by itself every night without your even trying, and you just have to write them down.

Building Your Story's House

Once you're thinking as a writer on a regular basis, you may still experience times when an idea just won't cohesively form a story. Oftentimes, writing isn't flowing because the idea isn't fully hatched.

Building a story is a lot like building a house. You have to start by pouring in your foundation—the basement. Trying to build on an unfinished basement is, perhaps, the most common cause for writer's block; it means you haven't done enough research. "Research" is a word easily associated with nonfiction work—you know exactly what it means in that context, right? It means you have to read up on your subject, conduct interviews, maybe visit the scene—it's pretty black and white. If you're experiencing writer's block when writing a nonfiction piece, it probably means you haven't developed enough of a basement yet.

"I believe the seeds for the thing called 'writer's block' are sown way before it shows up," says screenwriting instructor Hank Isaac. "I tell my writing students that being stuck with nowhere to go and nothing to say usually means one thing: either the story or characters (or both) are not clear. The writing part was begun too soon, before there was that needed clarity. Because if the characters are understood and the story—even the simple form of it—is understood, there's nothing there to stop a writer from moving forward."

Ask yourself this: if there were a pop quiz on your subject tomorrow, how would you score? If you can't confidently answer that you'd get an A, then you need to do more research. Talk to people who are experts on your subject. Don't be afraid to ask them for explanations where you need it.

While writing an article about radio shows for *Writer's Digest* today, I had to humble myself and do just that—an interviewee had gone on at length about "drive-time radio shows," and although I had an idea this probably meant shows that air during rush hour, I wasn't 100 percent confident. A quick e-mail to the interviewee made me feel a lot better about my potential pop-quiz score.

In fiction, however, research may sound like a foreign concept. Sure, it means you should know about the area and time period you're writing about, but it also means so much more than that.

In just the same way that you would interview a businessman for a nonfiction profile for a magazine, you can and should interview your characters for short stories, novels, and scripts. How well do you know your characters? Do you know their favorite foods? Do you know what's in their closets that they can't bear to part with even though they'll probably never use those things again? Or how they feel about their high school reunions? Or where they took their favorite vacation?

Sit down and have a conversation with your characters. (Doing so out loud is a great way to ensure you get your own seat on a public bus.) Ask them about their hopes and dreams, their failures, passions, pet peeves, insecurities, relationships, childhoods, greatest losses, and hobbies. Ask them *why*. Why do they care about their friends? Why are they so afraid of public speaking? Why do they have trouble sleeping?

Write it all down. Wait until you know your character as well as you know your mother, siblings, or best friend. Wait until you can finish this character's sentences. That's how you build the basement for your house. You pour that concrete in, inch by inch, until you've got a foundation strong enough to hold the rest of the house you're going to build.

A second method for "basement building" is to call a friend and tell him all about your piece. Just the act of having to summarize your story on the spot should show you where the gaps lie and where you're most unsure of yourself. Your friend should feel free to poke holes in your presentation and ask questions; that will help you find out how an audience might perceive your story. If you don't have a friend who will listen to your ramblings, then write out a short summary of your story. Join a writer's group (there are lots of them on-line, if you can't find an in-person one—see chapter 18) and pass it to them, asking them to tell you if it all sounds clear.

If you don't feel comfortable doing this, you can talk into a tape recorder instead, or call your own answering machine and tell yourself the story. Then listen to it and try to determine where you slow down, sound unsure of yourself (listen for "umms"), or skip parts of the story. These are the areas that need to be developed.

Once you've got the basement, you can build the structure of the house. Each scene of your story is a room in this ever-expanding abode. There must be points of interest and a reason for each room. If you find that one room is serving no particular purpose, knock it down. I don't care if it's pretty; each scene must propel the story forward and teach us something new. If it doesn't, get rid of the room.

Now look at the rest of the house. Does it have windows? If not, you haven't given readers a peek into your story yet. It may be too abstract or personal; you haven't yet chosen to share your vision with an audience in a way that they can access. There's absolutely nothing wrong with writing for yourself, but if you're writing for an audience, you've got to make sure you've given the reader the right to look around inside your house. Those windows have to be opened wide so the reader can crawl inside your brain and have a comfortable visit with the story and characters you've created. Give them something to relate to, give them characters they can care about, and let them in on the details that make your invented world realistic.

Next, build yourself a chimney. A chimney, especially with smoke wafting out of it, means you see this house as a real place with real people living in it. If you don't feel that way, you haven't given your story a heartbeat yet. You have to be so enmeshed in your story that it feels real, or you can't expect anyone else to believe it's real. Spark up that fire in the fireplace and bring some life into your story.

▶ PROMPT: Describe your life in terms of themes. If you could choose one theme that reflected your early childhood, what would it be? What's your theme now?

Characters Count

Although we must be alone while we're in the act of writing, that doesn't mean we're antisocial people. In fact, perhaps more than any other purveyor of the arts, writers love people. Think about it: it's not really what we write about that's important, it's *who* we write about. This is true for writers of fiction and nonfiction, books and articles, poems and stories. Our ultimate goal is to entertain, educate, and possibly even uplift *people.*

Characters are a writer's stock in trade. They populate our stories, fill our imaginary settings, wear our carefully described expressions. They take on lives of their own: eating, drinking, jogging, flying space shuttles, operating on beating hearts, or just moseying on down to the fishing hole with their best friends.

So if you've gone over your pros-and-cons list and can't quite figure out what is at the very heart of your writer's block, perhaps it's not even a *what* at all—but a *who.*

To find out, ask yourself this: if your characters were at a party, which ones would you be dying to talk to? Upon whose conversations would you desperately want to eavesdrop? With whom would you fall in love?

Your characters need not, *should* not, be perfect human beings. But they must have what the *American Idol* judges call the

"X-factor." The X-factor is that special something that compels you to watch that person. I think Angelina Jolie is full of X-factor. Would you want her to be your best friend and come to your house for Thanksgiving dinner? No, maybe not. But are you glued to the television when she appears on a talk show, or driven to scan through articles about her quirky personal habits? If Angelina doesn't float your boat, think of other celebrities who fascinate you. There's no simple formula for making a character compelling—you'll only know you've succeeded if you can't stop watching what he or she does next.

In her article series *Ten Tips on Creativity*, writing instructor Emily Hanlon talks about how to "fall down the rabbit hole" in your writing life. How do you know if you're there? "You see your character's flaws, but no longer judge them," she writes. "You love your character despite his flaws, you love him for his flaws, you love, you are in love, and the real magic can begin. You no longer try to stop or change the character. You are passionately along for the ride."

When you haven't created characters who are irresistible to you, the writing inevitably becomes tedious. You *try* to make them interesting rather than just allowing them to be themselves. If you ever catch yourself making a character do something wild like skydiving or rushing into a burning building, it's probably a sign that your character wasn't intriguing enough on her own. Either reconsider that character's makeup, or chuck her and find someone else to step into the role.

Meeting New Characters

Perhaps your cabinet has run dry of fascinating characters. Maybe your stable of beautiful heroines and dashing heroes or rumpled detectives and damsels in distress has been depleted by your last big push to meet a deadline or wrap up chapter 78.

If so, it may be time to get out of your rut, take a shower, trade in your writer's sweats for a pair of comfy jeans and some walking shoes, and hit the bricks.

Go someplace populated, crowded, noisy, busy. Yes, it's quite a shocking change from your writing space, but the payoff is well worth the investment.

Bring a disposable camera. Bring a sketch pad, or just a legal pad and several pens. Bring a tape recorder and use it to describe not what, but who you run into (after apologizing, of course). Or bring a camcorder and play it back for yourself on your VCR later. The homeless guy on the corner might turn into your next heartwarming hero. The pimply-faced kid behind the TCBY counter might become your serial killer's next victim—or even your next serial killer. The shop clerk who snubs you, the grandma you help up the escalator, the stalker who follows you into Spencer's—these are all potentially great characters.

Every writer needs a cast of characters to draw on in moments of desperation, and perhaps your writer's block is begging you to add to your current stable. Going out in public is one way to stock your pantry full of people you can describe when the occasion arises.

Pay attention to their faces, their hair, their wardrobes, their dialects, their phraseologies, their walks, their laughs, their mannerisms. Devour the details, feast on the minutiae, take it all in, and then take in some more. Exhaust yourself in the process of recording them all or just committing them to memory. Stay away from your desk for a whole day if you need to, or several days, for that matter.

The payoff may come tonight, when you're so jazzed up to write about a stranger you've discovered, or it may come a year from now, when you least expect to remember that brief encounter you had with someone who perfectly fills the shoes of a character in your future novel. The world is full of characters, in every sense of the word, and you might just be surprised by how fascinating your fellow man and woman can be.

Broadcastus Interruptus

When you're blocked, it's often more tempting than ever to close your notebook, unplug your typewriter, or log off your computer, and veg out in front of the boob tube with a bag of chips. Ah, to let someone else do the thinking for you for a change. What a treat.

But why not turn Must-See-TV into another form of therapy for your writer's block? To accomplish this heroic feat, pick up your notebook and your favorite brand of pens or pencils. Then, the next time you're enjoying your favorite sitcom or that predictable movie of the week, turn the TV off during the last five to ten minutes. (Come on, you know what was going to happen anyway!)

Just click it off, close your eyes, open up your notebook—and finish it. Finish the sitcom, finish that new Danielle Steel movie on Lifetime, finish that bag of chips.

What would the main character do? What would the villain say? How would you resolve the conflict? What would your climax be? What would your zingers be? What would happen just before you fade out? And how would you bring all those lovable TV characters back to life next week?

This prime-time exercise may seem trivial, but you just may be surprised by how quickly your pen flies across the page as you seal the fates of your favorite TV characters. And don't forget, you're not just having fun—you're *writing*.

If one night isn't enough to get you unblocked, try again the next night. And the next. If it helps, turn the TV off sooner and sooner—and pick up your pen earlier and earlier—each night. Or don't even turn the TV on at all. Write your own movie of the week or half-hour sitcom, starring your own lovable characters who spring to life among the fields of your fertile imagination.

Just don't try this trick when you've got a house full of people watching the last two minutes of the Super Bowl!

6

Kicking the Critic Off His Pedestal

Your Inner Critic

"My inner critic? Her voice varies," says Sabina C. Becker. "On a good day, she sounds like me in my incarnation as a poetry editor for www.netauthor.org. On a bad day, she sounds like me as a little girl: 'I'm siiiiiick. My stomach hurts. I hate this junk. I can't write. Can I just sit and veg, huh, Mummy, huh, huh?' And on a *really* bad day, she sounds like Sylvia Plath, talking from the inside of a gas oven."

Your inner critic is a part of you. It's the self-doubting, pessimistic, obnoxious part that thinks writing is a silly profession and that you have no business ever picking up a pen. I'd tell you to just ignore it, but we all know it's not that easy. It's like trying to ignore a mother-in-law who keeps reminding you that you're a lousy cook, and why don't you iron her son's socks once in a while? After all, *she* used to.

Your critic is another part of your soul that has been forged in childhood: the parent with a stove full of boiling pots who didn't have time for your new story and said, instead, "That's nice, dear." The classmate who told you your short story was disgusting because it had a kissing scene. Even the gym coach who said you couldn't do twenty-five chin-ups (and proved himself right) or the school bully who never picked you to be on his team.

All of these jabs are notches on the critic's ever-expanding belt, and serve to erode your confidence—especially when it comes to your writing.

Turn the critic into a character, pretending you're about to write a story about him. But before you have him get run over by a bus, ask him why he's so darn creepy. Find out why he hates your writing so much. Ask him where these thoughts came from, and you may just find out he's a composite of a number of people in your life: your mother who thinks you should have been a doctor, your English teacher who gave you lousy grades because you couldn't spell and didn't follow rules well, your uncle who keeps asking when you're going to get a real job (before he goes off to collect his unemployment benefits), your neighbor who wants to know what you do in your house all day long, and every editor who's ever rejected your work without offering an explanation, leaving your mind to dream up a thousand reasons why you couldn't hold a candle to all those Real Writers who never get rejected. (By the way—it only seems that way. Most professional writers had their work rejected repeatedly before they ever got an acceptance, and most of us continue to get rejections no matter how far along in our careers we are. Writers who don't get rejections aren't Real. They're Imaginary.)

▶ PROMPT: Write about your character's attachment to an inanimate object.

Who Is Your Critic?

I think of my critic as a conglomerate of Statler and Waldorf from the Muppets, sitting in their balcony and throwing tomatoes at Fozzie Bear while he was doing his best to deliver a comedy routine. Yep, I've got my own personal heckler who chucks imaginary fruit at me while I write. Lucky for me, I have a great raincoat that I don whenever I hunker down at the keyboard. Every writer should have one. The tomatoes wash right off.

What does your critic look like? Get to know him and his motivations and agenda. Find his weak spots. Realize he can only bother you if you let him.

Who Is Your Advocate?

Now create a new character in your mind: the advocate. The advocate loves every word you write. The advocate thinks you are the embodiment of sheer brilliance and every word that comes from your pen or keyboard is golden. Whenever the critic gets loud, let the advocate step up to the plate and reduce the critic to a quivering little baby. If it helps, your advocate can be played by Arnold Schwarzenegger.

The advocate should counter every negative thought with a positive one, like a little devil on one shoulder and an angel on the other. When the critic says, "Your writing is stupid," the advocate says, "Your writing is going to make a difference in people's lives." And then he drives the critic into the ground cartoonstyle, until only his head is visible.

Let them argue it out on paper; let the critic say whatever he wants, but always let the advocate have the last word. The advocate knows the real you. He speaks the truth, whereas the critic just tries to trip you up because he's jealous of the fact that you're bold enough to take creative risks. Critics are usually mathematicians. They don't have a creative bone in their bodies and wouldn't know great writing if it whacked them on the head (which, incidentally, is just what you should do to your critic—in your mind, that is, unless you like looking like a weirdo who's whacking herself in the head).

The only way the critic has any power is if you believe him, at least a little, in that niggling little back-of-the-brain spot where you think maybe your writing is worthless, and maybe it is silly to get into this profession when you could be doing something sensible instead—like boring yourself to tears at a day job in exchange for a guaranteed amount of money each week.

You have to have a little more faith in your advocate. Trust him. He wouldn't lie to you. You are good, and the more writing you do, the better you'll get. The longer the critic interferes with your ability to write, uninhibited, the longer it will take you to reach your potential. You must—wait, I'll repeat that more emphatically—you *must* be able to take chances, write your brains out, go further than you thought you could go, and write some utter garbage along the way.

The poet William Stafford once said, "There is no such thing as writer's block for writers whose standards are low enough."

Now I'm not suggesting that you quit caring about the quality of your finished works; what I am suggesting is that you quit caring about the quality of your first drafts, and even your second drafts. Lower those standards. Decide you're going to be the Yugo of writing. If you happen to be brilliant by accident, well, fine. But there's no need for brilliance today. Today, you just want to be a Yugo. You can be a Porsche later.

How to Quiet the Critic

A good way to quiet the critic is to begin your writing first thing—and I do mean *first* thing—when you wake up, while you're still groggy. If you have trouble getting used to the idea of allowing yourself to write garbage, this is likely to help you along. You can't help but write garbage while you're half asleep. This probably won't be your most inspired work, but the trick here is to keep going and transit through your increasing alertness. Don't stop to get coffee, or you're likely to interrupt the hazy, critic-free state. Commit to your badness. If you're going to write badly, go all the way. A body in motion tends to stay in motion, so you have a good shot of keeping the momentum going when you're awake enough to write more coherently.

If you still can't turn off your critic's yammering, then turn off your computer monitor while you type, so your critic can't see what you're writing. This will reduce your tendency to reread passages and edit as you go along. Sure, you'll make some typos, but who cares? You've blinded the critic. You won. (Insert maniacal laughter here.)

In describing her battle with manic-depressive illness, Patty Duke said she didn't want to take medication because while it could eliminate the really low lows, it would also steal the very high highs. That's just my point about the critic. If you hang onto him, yes, he might just save you from writing garbage—but he'll also steal your flashes of brilliance. You have to make peace with every part of your writing: the brilliance and schlock alike. You're a one-person Odd Couple.

You have to stand up straight and audacious and proclaim, "I am brilliant, I am a hack, and I'm proud of all the words I write, because they're mine."

Rehabilitate Your Critic

Now, make an agreement with the critic. Tell him that you're putting him in the time-out corner until he comes up with something constructive to say. Stick a dunce cap on his head and turn a deaf ear to his protests. He can just sit there in the corner forever if he can't learn to be helpful.

You may want to make a physical manifestation of the critic. Your critic may be a rock, an ugly stuffed animal, an origami dragon—whatever shape best represents it to you. When it's appropriate, lock your critic away. Literally hide him, banish him from your sight.

But if you believe that people can change, then believe that your critic can change.

Your critic has to take some time away to let the advocate's teachings sink in. He doesn't belong anywhere near you during your first draft, but he can be useful later on if he learns to behave. When you're rewriting and revising, you can let the critic out of the corner and ask for his suggestions. He might just have something useful to say underneath that brash exterior.

Certainly, you've looked back on some of your early writings and wanted to cringe. How childish, how clichéd, how melodramatic, how undercooked those stories were! But that doesn't mean that you shouldn't have been proud of them when you wrote them; don't take that away from yourself. You can't divorce yourself from your bad writing because without it you'd never have made progress. And any money you made from your writing would be blown on alimony payments.

▶ PROMPT: Use the "found words" technique. Look around you right now and pick out five words you see. For example, I see the word "twice" on a medicine bottle, "formatted" on a box of computer disks, "nutrition" on a water bottle, "golf" on a book spine, and "function" on my phone. Use the five words you find in your next story.

Speak to Yourself Like a Friend

Just as nearly every musician had to start with scales and off-tune renditions of "Row, Row, Row Your Boat," you should consider those early writings your practice time. Maybe you hit some real squeakers, your tempo fell apart, and you brought your instructor to tears, but you were learning those basic skills and finding your voice. Even better, you were showing discipline and taking a risk. Yes, even those earliest writings were worthy of applause.

Paul Foxman, the psychologist who coauthored my book, *Conquering Panic and Anxiety Disorders,* said something that applies to just about every area of life: "Never say anything to yourself that you wouldn't say to a good friend."

Absorb that.

Unless you're a sociopath, you'd never tell your good friend that her writing was trite, hackneyed, boring, unoriginal, or any other variation that hits home with you. Now become your own best friend and speak to yourself in only constructive terms.

This doesn't mean you have to blow sunshine up your own derriere. Quite the opposite—if you expect your writing to really resonate with people, you'll have to go through a tough round of editing down the line. But even then, there's no room for insults. There's a world of difference between "my writing stinks" and "this paragraph isn't clear."

Learn to speak to yourself kindly, even when you're allowing the critic to step in. To ensure that he doesn't get tossed back to the time-out corner make him promise that every word out of his mouth will only serve to improve, not insult, your writing.

When he's on his best behavior, a strong inner critic can become your best friend—he can help you to see the weak spots in your writing and he can keep after you until your work is as good as it can possibly be. He can even help you to part with a piece that just isn't working. If he came with pizza, he'd be perfect.

Don't Get Stuck on the Wrong Words

You can (and should) get feedback from a wide variety of sources: writing groups, editors, agents, friends, a microphone too close to the speaker, but in the end, it's just you and your critic who can decide which words are the best ones to serve your purpose.

When you're working on your first draft, you may not find just the right words, and that's fine. If you're like me, you may get stuck on a phrase, thinking, "That's just not quite right. That's not exactly what I mean," or "That's a cliché," or "I can't repeat that word/phrase again." What I generally do here is to first call out to my fiancé, "Hey! What's a better way of saying, 'She felt overwhelmed?'" If he doesn't spit out a brilliant response in about five seconds, it's time to skip it and come back to it later. I'd suggest you do the same, but he gets hassled enough by me.

Switch to caveman language in this situation. Just write it in the most basic way you can ("Seanna felt overwhelmed by all the things she had to do"), then bracket the phrase, sentence, or word you want to fix later and just leave it. If you're at a total loss, type any random capital letters (e.g., NNNNN) to signal yourself that something needs to be filled in there (or when you want another way to say "constipated"). If you still can't come up with the right wording later on, ask for feedback. I call my mom (a former English teacher) or bug my writer friends. I'm also fond of using the thesaurus for word replacements—and if I'm on the computer, I go to www.rhymezone.com, a very handy site that you can use to find rhymes, similar words, definitions, antonyms, and more.

When you're finished with a piece and ready to let it out into the world, lock up that critic again because he's the king of cruel hindsight. He'll only nag you and tell you that the work wasn't really ready. Instead, give the advocate center stage and let him lavish praise on you, congratulate you on a job well done, and buy you drinks.

However, there may come a time when two isn't enough and you need *three* for company. When your critic is too harsh and your advocate is too forgiving, sometimes you need to haul out the missing link of your literary triumvirate: the pragmatist. (Otherwise known as "the realist.")

In Case of Emergency, Call on the Pragmatist

Think of the pragmatist as the referee who intercedes when your critic and advocate have come to blows or are no longer speaking to you. While your critic may say something harsh like, "That stinks," and your advocate may say something poetic like, "That's a diamond lurking in the rough," the pragmatist will often say something like, "Even Hemingway looked forward to a good rewrite." Of course, your pragmatist should have a bigger repertoire because after the twentieth time you hear "Even Hemingway looked forward to a good rewrite," you'll be ready to deck him.

A hybrid of your best friend's Jewish mother and your favorite priest, the pragmatist won't come out often, just when you need him the most. Like right now. When you're blocked, running scared, and looking for quick fixes and easy ways out. The pragmatist doesn't have all the answers, but usually he makes pretty good sense.

Let the pragmatist be the little voice inside you that wants you to think about writing anything you want, but wants you to think twice. The pragmatist will tell you to revise, revise, revise, but also not to dwell on things too long before you suck out all the passion and life from them. The pragmatist may be the gentle voice of reason, but he never forgets he's in the employ of that strange and magical creature, The Writer.

(That's you, by the way.)

7

Your Ugly Notebook

I want you to buy an ugly notebook.

Pretty notebooks and journals make you feel like you have to write important and polished things in them. Ugly notebooks let you be yourself in whatever condition you're in. Oh, and be a cheapskate. Don't you dare buy one of those gold-trimmed-page journals.

Now, give your notebook a name. Mine's named Stanley.

In this notebook, I want you to write stupid things. Trivial, pointless, everyday details that fall out of your brain when you're eating breakfast. I want there to be ketchup stains and coffee rings all over this notebook.

This is not the same as journaling, so you'll have to unlearn that urge. By all means, keep a separate journal (or diary, whichever term you prefer), but don't let this ugly notebook become one.

In a journal, you're probably trying to record your feelings and how you perceive the world around you in a coherent, orderly fashion so that you may later look back and see what an erudite, clever person you've always been. Think of the ugly notebook as your journal's drunken cousin.

This drunken cousin is sometimes an embarrassment to the family, and you'd prefer that no one ever associate you with him. After all, you're sophisticated and articulate, and this cousin is just a babbling idiot with stains on his shirt. (You might name your notebook "Cletus" or something.)

But deep down, you love your cousin. And when nobody's looking, you and he share plenty of laughs, because you can let it all hang out around him.

▶ PROMPT: Write about a wedding your character doesn't want to attend.

How to Use This Notebook

The point of this notebook is to let you jot down every little thing that pops into your brain, without any censoring whatso-ever, until you feel creatively purged and ready to focus.

Sometimes, writer's block is not caused by a lack of ideas, but too many ideas all vying for attention at once. You get scattered and don't know where to start. This notebook will help you filter.

Just stick your pen on the top of the page and write. If you've got nothing to write about, write about why you don't have any-thing to write about. Write about how you feel right now, and what you're doing and seeing, and all of the things around you demanding a piece of you.

In her book *The Artist's Way*, Julia Cameron advocates the use of "morning pages." In essence, the rules of morning pages are that you must write three throw-away pages every morning.

But you already know how I feel about rules, especially that "you-must-write-every-day" rule. So here's my "un-rule": write in your ugly notebook whenever you damn well feel like it. You can write three paragraphs or ten pages at a time, and you can do it at any time, in any place, in crayon, in marker, working back to front, or filling in pages at random, while hanging upside down from a tree with no clothes on (I do *not* want to know where you keep your pen).

Filling this notebook should never feel like a chore. It's supposed to be something you look forward to doing, so don't let it become a dentist's appointment. Don't use guilt to prod yourself into writing in it. Don't feel like Real Writers would fill their notebooks faster than you do (though, yes, they'd probably do it fully clothed). This is your spot to be you, to write about whatever thoughts are pinballing around in your brain, and to enjoy your oasis. No pressure. You're a writer no matter what happens in this ugly notebook. You're a writer, you're a writer, you're a writer. Put that in your notebook and smoke it.

Sometimes my thoughts don't come out in words. Sometimes they come out in cartoons. I'm particularly fond of my pictures of a cracked-open head with a person eating her own brain with a fork and a cartoon bubble over the top proclaiming, "Yum." I think the makers of *Hannibal* stole my old notebook, because I drew it years before the film. It might have been inspired by the Stephen Crane poem that starts with the line "In the desert" ("But I like it / Because it is bitter, / And because it is my heart").

I want you to write in colors. Markers, crayons, or colored pens and pencils all work. I want song lyrics to creep in there, and bubble letters, and too many exclamation points!!! I want you to use all the excessive punctuation you want, like you have an endless supply of dots and lines stored under your desk.

Don't lift your pen from the page, and don't stop writing until you're done. Write your brains out. Don't think of it as practice, and don't try to hone your skills, improve as you go along, or write rough drafts of stories you're actually planning to write. If new story ideas happen to wrangle their way into your ugly notebook, all the better, but that's not the point. You're stretching your muscles and warming up.

When to Use Your Notebook

Have you ever watched a dancer do all those crazy contortions before she actually starts dancing? Or listened to a singer vocalize all those wacky noises before singing? It's not pretty. The noises usually sound like tongue twisters set to scales, and the singer stretches out her mouth, purses her lips, flips her tongue, and makes yawning noises.

They do this every time before performing. They don't stop because they get good. You never get too good for warm-ups.

Your ugly notebook can be a warm-up, a refresher, or both. You can choose to use it only when you're blocked, or you can use it every day before or in the middle of your "real" writing. I like to use it when I start to feel drained in the middle of an assignment. It wakes me up and gives me a second wind.

Using Free Association

One of the benefits of writing continually without picking up your pen from the paper is that your subconscious thoughts will find their way to the page. You'll see words come out that you didn't even know were hiding there in your head, and not just swear words. You'll find thoughts you thought you had buried long ago. You'll find things that are demanding to be written, even when you told them "no." Give yourself permission to write things that don't make sense. Let yourself follow whims and tangents.

This is known as "free association," and it was the method Sigmund Freud used in psychoanalysis. He reported that patients became so relaxed that strong, emotional memories often came out during sessions. Don't be surprised if the same happens in your ugly notebook. You may plan to write about the bird outside your window and end up writing about the death of your high school friend without ever meaning to.

Don't be stingy with space; let those words pour out as big and as undercooked as they are. Don't stop to correct your spelling or reread any of what you've written. If you don't have a feel for when you're through, you may want to set a timer for five or ten minutes to start.

When you've finished, check to see if you're ready to work on a "real" project, one that might actually see the light of day.

▶ PROMPT: You have just discovered you have only one month to live. What will you do with this time?

Making Up Writing Games

Writer Pati Mills broke out of writer's block by making up a game. "All year in 1999, I carried two blank journals, and when I was out waiting with a friend, I would draw her into this little game I created." First, each person had to pick a headline out of the newspaper and write it on top of a page. This became the title for a short story. Then they'd each pick twelve words—any words that popped into their heads. Finally, they'd switch books. She'd use her friend's headline and words, and her friend would use hers to create a short story with a beginning, middle, and end in only five minutes. (This is how most newspaper stories are now written.) At the end of the game, she gifted each friend with the book and short story they wrote to use as their journal for the remainder of the year.

"So much joy came from doing this with old and new friends that I started writing short stories regularly," she said. She loved reliving the laughter they had shared as they read stories aloud to each other.

You can use the prompts in this book, or make up your own writing games. And remember, one can never have too many ugly notebooks.

It sounds a little pompous, but generally speaking, I don't suffer from writer's block. When I sit at the keyboard my mind can be a complete blank—I may have nothing planned whatsoever—and I begin typing, and just let it flow. What I write may be utter codswallop, but by dint of constant hacking and cutting I eventually get an idea of what small gem might actually be lurking in the prose, and I then work to bring that to the fore.

On the odd occasion that I do get stumped, I have a fallback remedy that usually works quite well: I take a shower. Nice and hot, for as long as I want to be in there. I frequently stand there for forty minutes or more, my eyes closed, letting my mind wander as it will.

Usually, something will materialize and I'll be running around looking for my Psion Revo [PDA] to jot it down. I carry my Revo everywhere with me, ever since I lost several great ideas as a result of not having something with me to jot them down. Inspiration, like some dreams, frequently yields ideas that are sometimes too fleeting to be left to a later debriefing.

—Peter G Q Brooks, writer

8

Self-Doubt and Other Stupid Garbage

Writer's block feeds on itself. First, you have one bad day where you stare at the blank page until you start hallucinating and seeing swirly shapes like the ones hypnotists use in old B movies, and then, you begin to fear that feeling.

So the next day comes, and you're even more anxious because you're afraid you're going to stare at that blank page again all day, hypnotized by the swirly shapes, and wind up acting like a chicken in front of complete strangers. And then the next day comes and you decide you've obviously taken a wrong career turn, and your guidance counselor was right when she said you should work in a shoelace factory. You decide Real Writers would never stare at a blank page for three days (or if they did, they'd write a great story about it, with the option of selling the film rights), which makes you a Fake Writer. Then you notice the veins in your hands are rather unappealing and your knees protrude and make creaking noises when you bend them. You have been made wrong. You are defective. Pity, because if you weren't so defective, you probably could have performed the simple act of filling a page with letters.

Don't think I'm going to correct you. Your knees probably do protrude, not that I noticed. I'm bowlegged, personally, and possess a cornucopia of stunning mental illnesses. If I weren't so defective in the first place, I'd probably never be a writer. After all, what sane and balanced human being would let her ability to eat be determined by the chance her brain would emit words worthy of publication day after day?

Writers come in all shapes and sizes, but we all pray for normalcy: "Just let me be like everyone else. Just let me fit in. Just let me run across a bag lady without wanting to record her entire life story. Just let me break up with a girl without writing her a thirty-two-page letter explaining why. Just this once, let me not feel so odd, so weird, so different."

But the world needs us weirdoes. If we didn't write about the glorious lives of bag ladies, mountain climbers, misfits, barflies, and homecoming queens, who would?

So go right ahead and be defective and write anyway. Write because you're defective. Write to distract yourself from your defectiveness. After all, without our defects, how would we ever be good writers?

▶ PROMPT: Describe a guilty pleasure of yours.

Stop Being So Serious

One of the ways that writers create anxiety in the first place is by separating work from play. Some writers think that the short stories they wrote as kids were play, but now they must put all that behind them and start being serious. They're going to work, and it's not going to be any fun, because Real Writers always have their brows furrowed and angry glasses of booze on hand to take the edge off of their pressure-laden, blood-sucking writing sessions.

The truth is that today's writing is merely an extension of those childhood days; your writing can be just as freewheeling, imaginative, and enjoyable as it was then. You just have to allow it to be. To prove it to yourself, drink lemonade and eat alphabet soup while you're working. Listen to the Muppets' theme song. Surround yourself with rainbow pencil mugs, *Star Wars* action figures, those wind-up chattering teeth, and other assorted curios of youth, whimsy, and delight.

Many writers feel that they need to be organized to be efficient, and this is good advice. Those twenty minutes it takes you to find a manila file folder's worth of much-needed research are twenty minutes you could have spent writing. But that doesn't mean you can't doodle peace signs and broken hearts all over that research folder. Or put a bumper sticker on your printer ("If you can read this, you're out of paper"). Or one of those wiggling hula girls on top of your computer monitor. Or use a *Baywatch* screen saver. Or . . . well, you get the picture.

You Owe It to the World to Outwit Your Block

Now, to be realistic, not every moment of your writing life is going to be a cartwheeling heap of joy. Some of it will feel more like childbirth. But remember that you've made the choice to write because it brings you some kind of pleasure. Zero in on that, and psychically connect with your ancestors who told stories around campfires for enjoyment.

Remember that you are not just one writer waging a war of words with the rest of the world, but that you are part of a grand tradition of troubadours and prophets, oracles and soothsayers. You are linked with wise Romans and brave Indian warriors.

While your tool may be a laptop and a cup of Joe, the tools of your ancestors were chunks of charcoal used to scribble on cave walls and quill pens held in ink-stained fingers.

You are not alone, nor are you fighting for an unworthy cause. Without the words—the *words*—of ancient writers, there would be no Ten Commandments, no tales of Cleopatra or Bathsheba, no Romeo, no Juliet, no gripping tales of Gettysburg or Shiloh, no *Diary of Anne Frank*, no *A Tree Grows in Brooklyn*, no *Roots*, no *Fast Times at Ridgemont High*, no *Color Purple*, no *Angela's Ashes*.

So you see, you don't just owe it to yourself to outwit writer's block—you owe it to history.

Secondary Gains from Writer's Block

In psychological terms, when a person gets some kind of benefit from a seemingly negative condition, it's called a "secondary gain." A person with panic disorder might be getting secondary gains because her husband pays more attention to her, or because she doesn't have to be responsible for things that might cause panic attacks—things like grocery shopping or banking. If she didn't want to do these things anyway, then she's actually getting some kind of a benefit from her illness and she might be reluctant to work at "curing" herself, even on a subconscious level, because she doesn't want to lose those benefits.

Think hard about what secondary gains you're getting from your writer's block. Is it saving you from the possibility of rejection? Does it make other people say kind things to you, and treat you with encouragement? ("Yes, but I wish they wouldn't pat me on the head and say 'good boy' over and over.") Does it allow you to pretend your writing skills are better than they are—"if only" you could get over the block? Does it shelter you from ever having to get feedback on your work or deal with an editor who may change your words?

Your block may be a form of self-preservation. If you're cruel to yourself about your writing talents, then your block may be your way of saving yourself from criticism. If most of your self-talk is about how you're untalented, unworthy, or unpublishable, then your block may exist so you can't be proven right. After all, if there is no writing, then there's nothing to criticize.

Perfectionism in Disguise

On the flip side, you may be avoiding writing because you've set in your mind that you're such a splendid writer you can't live up to your own expectations. "Procrastination is perfectionism in disguise," says Dr. Paul Foxman. "Many of my patients have described blocks that appear to be the result of perceiving that their work will not meet their own high standards."

Take the risk. Be willing to lose control and to open up all those doorways in the dark recesses of your mind. There may be brilliance in the darkness just waiting for you to shine a light on it.

You have to make it worthwhile to give up the secondary gains. Decide that you're going to take your medicine. Giving up your writer's block may subject you to some scary or unpleasant feelings, but if you never give it up, you'll never find out how high you can fly. Make the conscious choice to let go of your block. Tell yourself you're ready to open yourself up to whatever may come as a result of your writing.

Writer, Compare not Thyself

Writer's block can also strike when you get caught up in comparing yourself to other, usually famous, writers. "Writer's block strikes when I read something similar to my own style and preferred topic but which is far more brilliant and graceful than anything I have ever written in my life," says freelance writer

Jennifer Durbin. "Makes me want to just go slit my own throat and be done with it. It is like comparing Cary Grant to William Shatner—one is sexy, smooth, and seamless, the other bearable, but just barely. There is no mistaking which is which.

"This is when I torture myself for ever having learned to put one word together with another to form a coherent sentence, for having gotten the writing bug in the first place, for ever having learned to turn on the computer, for ever having learned to read. Oh why, oh why can't that other dazzling writer just get hit by a nice train? Why can't I create such symbolism? At these times I promise I will never again read another word by Madame Dazzling. But it is like a bad car crash on the side of the road—I can't keep myself from looking. I see that name on a byline and I am a moth to the flame—up in smoke.

"Then it occurs to me—William Shatner gets hired anyway. William Shatner doesn't have to be, isn't expected to be Cary Grant. Ever. Then I go off and read a few published words by somebody, anybody, who isn't Madame Dazzling and I remind myself that this person got hired, got published, and I am every bit as good. But, frankly, this feat once took years to accomplish. In the interim, Madame Dazzling published three more books, two of them made into movies, while I languished in lower management. My only advice: Compare not Thyself."

Aha! I couldn't have said it any better. It's easy to see other writers' strengths and believe you're not worthy of disinfecting their toilet tanks. Humor writer Felice Prager (www.write-funny.com) had some of the same thoughts after reading Wally Lamb's *I Know This Much Is True*. She spent an entire summer obsessing about his writing and doing little else.

"I went into a severe 'I-am-not-a-writer' funk," she says. "I've fallen into this gloom a few times in my life. This time, it took more than a month for me to convince myself that it's not a competition, and what I write is not similar in style to what Wally Lamb or Barbara Kingsolver write. Good thing, or else the funk might have lasted forever.

"Yet, the funk rears its ugly head often enough. It sneaks up behind me when I'm rereading something I wrote and it says, 'You call *that* good writing?' It mumbles things to me like, 'Would Barbara Kingsolver be as impressed with your work as you are with hers?' and 'Would Wally Lamb want to reread sections of what you write like you do with his?'"

All of this masochism does have one benefit, however, according to Felice. "It makes me set the bar very high for myself. And I guess that's not a bad thing in the big picture."

Setting the bar high is wonderful. Setting it unrealistically high—say, Kareem Abdul Jabbar high—can paralyze you. It's important that as a writer you never aspire to *be* another writer. Surely, you can steal snippets of style and borrow interesting phraseology, but beware of trying to fill another writer's shoes (especially with cement). They're already filled, and when you try too hard to emulate another writer, you're really just copping out of finding your own voice.

Acquaintances rarely help the situation. There's always that family member you formerly liked who announces her revelation around the Thanksgiving dinner table: "Hey, Jenna, my kids are reading the *Harry Potter* series. Why don't you write something like that? You could sell a lot of books."

Oh. Why didn't I think of that? Of course, all I have to do is break into J. K. Rowling's computer, steal all her notes, and I'll be rolling in it.

▶ PROMPT: A young boy and a young girl hate each other. Write about why.

Turning Your Back on Books

It may be tempting to quit reading great writers' works altogether. You may proclaim that from now on, you will only read children's book reports and VCR instruction manuals poorly translated from Japanese. This, however, will not solve your crisis—you still won't be able to program the damn thing, and you'll still know that somewhere, somehow, Madame Dazzling is out there writing disgustingly glorious prose.

"Back in the days when I played tennis, a few kids deliberately chose weaker opponents so they could win," says humorist Bill Harper. "But it had the opposite effect—their playing standard actually came down to match their weaker opponent's. This is probably true in writing. Keep reading nothing but those VCR manuals, and soon you'll feel you'll never be able to write a VCR manual as good as the ones you're reading. Though we're not supposed to consider other writers our opponents, it's by reading better works that we push ourselves to excel."

Now I want you to repeat this phrase over and over until it sinks in: "I will never be Madame Dazzling . . . and *she will never be me.*"

Jealousy Begins at Home

But then there's the other kind of professional jealousy, the kind that arises when someone you know has a seemingly endless supply of good luck. A neophyte screenwriter straight out of college sells his first script for $600,000 against $1 million. Someone in your writing group lands a three-book deal. A friend from high school has her byline in *Cosmopolitan.* And you don't.

The jealousy monster turns a wretched shade of puke green when you start thinking to yourself, "But I write better than so-and-so!" There's even a good chance that you do. But for whatever reason, this person has hit the big time while you're still struggling to pay for your Ramen noodles with your writing earnings. Three more payments and you'll own another packet!

When the World Wide Web was still in its infancy, I made regular visits to a message board for children's writers. I had just begun writing picture books, and this particular destination seemed like a fun, clean place to receive inspiration and get motivated to not only write more, but to publish the books I'd written. I thought I'd get some tips from the pros, be able to ask a few questions, receive illuminating answers, and perhaps even make some contacts in the publishing field while I was at it.

That lasted about three weeks. The fact was there were only four regular posters in attendance. Unfortunately, these four ladies, all children's writers and publishing veterans, were just a tad *too* successful for my taste. Every day one of them published something new, or got a starred review in *Kirkus*, or signed another three-book deal, or had lunch with Beverly Cleary.

It started out as exciting. "Yay!" I'd scream. "Way to go, Bertha. Congrats. I knew you could do it." Or, "Another book deal, Eunice? You go, girl." By the end of my short-lived journey it was more like, "Swollen-headed weenie. If I walk into the bookstore and find a 'Bertha' section, I'll hurl on my shoes."

I admit it. I was jealous. I was also running out of clean shoes. But I wasn't alone. Many a flame erupted because several newbies like myself had the guts to ask the four amigas to let someone else brag for a minute. The only problem was, none of us could. Yet.

Unfortunately, this is another one of those feelings that never completely goes away, as far as I can tell. I consider myself a pretty successful writer, but I still get a twinge of jealousy when another writer I know trumps me in some way or another. I might even love this person, but God help her if her book reaches the best-seller list before mine does. The voodoo pins come out, and I spend all day whining to myself about how I deserve that best-seller spot more than she does. For goodness sake, she has a rich husband! She doesn't need the money. Besides, she barely made it through high school and still doesn't know the difference between "your" and "you're." She spends half her day at the beauty parlor and the other half at the gym. She's not a Real Writer!

Then comes the list of all the ways I've paid my dues, and how it would only be fair if my book sold at least a million copies. And if everyone who bought *her* book returned it, preferably stained with spittle.

Professional jealousy is completely normal.

Become Your Own Best Cheerleader

You would be surprised how many writers likely envy you already—or would, if they could read what you write. I don't even know you and yet, I'm sure that if I did, I'd find a good reason to be jealous of you, too. There is something special about the writing that can only come from you. Nurture your own talent. Be good to it. Nourish it with praise and pats on the back. Take the time to bask in your own glory. Wear plenty of sunscreen.

No matter whether every person who's ever read your work has turned inside out with excitement or whether no one's ever encouraged you much, you should become your own best cheerleader. Only you know your true potential, and only you can sit down and do the writing that will best tell the world what you really mean to share.

Even the most celebrated authors have their share of self-doubt and neuroses. Best-selling authors routinely worry that their next work will be ridiculed and the world will really discover that they've been faking it all along, that they have no legitimate talent, didn't graduate from any fancy writing schools, and just got lucky before.

I, on the other hand, am at peace with my inner hack. How about you?

Putting Your Writing into Perspective

"I love being a hack," says Pete Barnstrom, novelist and screenwriter. "If I ever start thinking that what I am writing is more important to anyone else than the least important thing in [his or her] life, I'll give it up. In fact, I think that would be a big contributor to writer's block, placing too much importance on the act of writing. It's just words on paper. If it's not fun, don't do it."

And perhaps, for you, outwitting writer's block is as simple as putting your writing into perspective. This tactic works for other fears, too, such as stage fright. I once had to do a radio show to support a story of mine that appeared in Adams Media Corporation's best-selling anthology series, *A Cup of Comfort*. Not having done many radio appearances at this stage of my career, I quickly gave a shout to one of my e-mail writing buddies who had done several such shows and asked her for some help.

Her advice was very simple: "Not to burst your bubble," she burst my bubble, "but don't make such a big deal about it. Honestly. Think about how intently *you* listen to the radio when you're driving to work. Especially a drive-time talk show! Unless your favorite song comes on, or a news bulletin from the president, how closely do you really listen? Chances are, not very closely. The same thing goes for your interview. I'll certainly be listening, but chances are *most people won't!*"

Voilà! End of stage fright, immediately. The interview went off without a hitch and I even got a callback for later that week and didn't stress once. What had changed? Nothing, except that I put the experience into proper perspective.

Get to know and appreciate whatever stage of the game you're in right now. You may be at beginner, intermediate, or advanced level. You may be returning after an extended break and have to catch up to where you were before. Wherever you are is where you are. That's why there are different weight classes in wrestling; a 90-pound boy isn't expected to wrestle a 180-pound boy. Don't stick yourself in the heavyweight category until you're ready. Excel in the lightweight category first. There are medals to be earned there.

▶ PROMPT: There's a great Garth Brooks song that goes, "Sometimes I thank God for unanswered prayers." Why might someone be thankful that a prayer wasn't answered? Write about a prayer you or your character has taken back.

Negative No More

For this week, I want you to write down all of the negative thoughts you have about your writing—then replace them with positive thoughts you can believe. This is a technique I learned from the *Attacking Anxiety* audio program, and I bet you'll be surprised by this exercise.

You may not believe you're a negative thinker until you start keeping track of all of your negative thoughts. Every time you think, "My writing is no good," "I'll never be published," "I'm not as good as so-and-so," or "I have no discipline," I want you to come up with a positive thought that replaces that thought. Then write it down. Don't go from one extreme to another—

"My writing is no good" doesn't have to become "I'm the greatest writer who ever lived." It can just become, "I'm just having trouble with this piece, but I'm a talented writer," or "My writing is improving every day."

You may be sabotaging your writing success by sending yourself negative messages all day long. When you tell a kid he's bad all the time, he becomes bad—even if he wasn't before. When you tell yourself you're a bad writer all the time, how will you ever free yourself up to become a good one?

The power of positive thinking can't be overemphasized. It's addictive, and you may find that it spills over into other areas of your life. Choose to be a positive person and to counter all of your negative thoughts with positive ones. Just try it for a week and see what you think at the end of it. And don't say I didn't warn you if you start singing in the rain and tiptoeing through the tulips while putting on a happy face.

If You Can Visualize It, You Can Do It

Some people find it very helpful to take the time to let their imaginations create an image of success before they begin working. What would success look like to you?

Next time you sit down to write, I want you to pause, close your eyes, and try this visualization. It might help if you read this section onto a cassette tape so you can keep your eyes closed and do the whole exercise without stopping to read.

Exercise:

Your writer's block is a huge, black, heavy, rectangular, or square object. When you close your eyes, all you can see is this big black block. Now I want you to see yourself standing in front of the block and disarming it. First I want you to change its color.

You may do so by waving a magic wand, or by sending the light that's inside you out into the block, or summoning the rain to wash away the black and turn it another color, whatever color signifies happiness to you.

Now I want you to change its shape. See how it's all hard and angular? I want you to soften its angles. You can't chip away at it, you can't force it. But you can use the power of your mind to change the block's consistency to a more gelatinous or sculptable material. Smooth down those edges until your block is no longer a block, but rather an oval, round, or free-formed shape. What do you see in the corners where the edges of the block used to be? Use your imagination and visualize what might be on the other side of the block. It should be idyllic and exciting. Of course, it's just a tease; you can't see the whole picture yet.

That's why you have to shrink the shape. You might pour water on it and watch it melt like the wicked witch in *The Wizard of Oz*, or you might inject it with a special shrinking agent. You might even give it a drink, à la *Alice's Adventures in Wonderland*'s "Drink me" bottle that made her shrink to only ten inches high. Watch that shape get smaller and smaller until it's only about a quarter of its original size.

Now what do you see? What's waiting for you on the other side of this block? Can you see yourself tearing open a carton from the mailman and finding stacks of your new book, fresh off the presses? Can you see yourself sitting at the premiere of your movie? Are you proudly thumbing through a magazine and finding your byline? Or handing a hand-bound story that you wrote to your grandchild?

It's so close now, and I want you to imagine it so well that your heart races in anticipation and all you want to do is run to that scene and savor it.

This block is no longer so menacing, is it? In fact, you're strong enough to pick it up. Go ahead. Walk to it, bend down, and lift it with both of your hands. Now give that block wings. Transform it into a butterfly and watch it fly away, dancing through the sky.

Nothing stands in your way anymore. You can now reach out and touch your dream. Go to that scene. Know that it is *you* standing there. *You* who can make this happen. *You* who holds the key to your own success.

This is not some far-off dream that only exists in your imagination. You can manifest whatever goal you visualize.

Now trace your steps back and visualize how you got there. You wrote. You sat down and created those pages, drawing from your passions and your creativity. You will write those pages today. You are on the right path to your dream. You will make this happen.

Writing for an Audience of One

When you write, do you have a particular audience in mind? "Sure I do," you say. "I'm writing for women who love mysteries." But now get more specific. Write for one person. Have her image in your mind. Better yet, cut out a photo in a magazine of a woman who looks like your target audience. Decide exactly who she is and what she likes. Write for her, specifically.

Don't write for your mother, or your teacher, unless they happen to be 100 percent supportive of your writing. If your mother would pass out in her cornflakes if she saw you use the word "crap," then you can't write for her. You have to write for someone you feel isn't judgmental at all, someone who desperately wants to read the story that you happen to be writing. That may be a sibling, a friend, or a stranger you've concocted. (Your mother may have told you never to talk to strangers, but she never said anything about writing for them.)

Picture his eyes widening when you reveal a new plot twist. Picture him laughing out loud with you, holding his breath, mouthing your words to himself. He delights in your every word. You can't let him down; if you wrote a grocery list, he'd think it was wonderful. (No, "grocery lists" is not a genre. Yet.) Write for him because he deserves to have the joyous experience of reading your work.

▶ PROMPT: Your main character has died unexpectedly, and you have been asked to give the eulogy. What will you say?

Write for a Reluctant Reader

It is a good idea to write for someone who doesn't read very often. I have a stable of friends who read fewer than five books a year. Does it mean they're illiterate? Boring? Unsophisticated? Not by a long shot. These are heavy-duty professionals who make every ounce of their brain matter—matter. They need to really fall in love with a book to finish it. And once they do, they finish it within days.

One of my most reluctant reading friends stumbled across Wally Lamb's first book, *She's Come Undone,* on my "borrowing bookshelf." Four days later, she had read it. *Twice.* That's the kind of reader I want to inspire: the reluctant reader. The reader who has no favorite authors. Who doesn't buy into the hype. Who doesn't follow talk show book clubs. Who just plain wants to read a good story. Who will hopefully give my book back to me (hint, hint). Period.

Sometimes it's easier to write for a genre audience. It's not that they're less demanding, it's just that they're more loyal. I have a friend who will read any old serial killer thriller that comes down the pike. Doesn't matter if it's a $7.99 paperback from one of today's biggest names, or a $4.99 cheese ball in the bargain bin. If it's got that tried-and-true "serial killer stalks victim while FBI profiler stalks serial killer—but who's stalking *him?*" formula, he's reading it. No doubt about it. (But whatever you do, don't sneak up on him—he's terribly paranoid.)

Do I want to write for this friend? Yes. But I would consider it a more crowning achievement if my more reluctant friend, that Wally Lamb fan, read *my* book.

Twice.

What to Do When You Don't Wanna

You may be stalled because you've hit a nerve with your writing. "Sometimes the passage is very difficult to write—the POV [point of view] character is enduring a situation similar to one that caused you great pain, and you're subconsciously putting off writing that painful scene," says writer T. M. Taylor. "Having writer's block is a sympathy-garnering excuse not to go through that painful place." Go there. Recognize that the most powerful scenes are usually the ones that were the hardest to write.

"Alternatively," she says, "the plot bunnies may be going somewhere you don't want to go, like when the plot calls for the death of a favorite character. Writer's block is a good excuse to frantically search your mind for a way to save said character while still getting your story finished."

If you're looking forward to killing off a "good" character, you're probably a little twisted. ("Put your hands up, and move away from the book. Slowly!") It's very natural for a writer to care about her characters as if they were real people. Chances are that they all contain a little bit of someone you knew, anyway. And you may not be too eager to have bad things happen to your good people.

If that's your problem, remind yourself of the greater good. Ask yourself how you're going to bring hope out of tragedy, or inspiration out of trauma.

Don't let your tragedies be tragic. (Huh?) Done correctly, they can be the most powerful, memorable, touching pieces of work. The ones that work typically share one thing in common: they aren't purely tragic. Although, by definition something terrible has to happen (usually the death of a main character), in the truly great tragedies something positive comes out of it.

Take the play *West Side Story*. Maria's brother kills Tony. Obviously a downer, unless you're that twisted guy who enjoys killing off the good characters. But if it ended with Tony lying bleeding on the ground, alone, we would have thrown our chocolate malt balls at the actors and walked out in anger. We all have enough sadness in real life. Why do we need one more piece of proof that life is bad? That's what the IRS is for.

But, no. *West Side Story* doesn't end there. Tony's death and Maria's anguish are the catalysts for positive change. For the first time, we see the two gangs mourning together and joining hand in hand to honor the deceased. The war is over. Tony was sacrificed, but it was for a greater good. That makes it a bittersweet ending, rather than just depressing.

Go ahead and dole out all the sadness you want, but throw us a lifeline at the end.

Fear of Success

Fear of success just amuses me. You may think the idea is silly—of *course* you want to be successful, right? Well, that depends on the Klingons you attach to the definition of success.

What of the screenwriter who dreads having to move to L.A. if he ever sells his script? Might he be impairing himself purposely, just because he equates success with moving to a place where you can really cut the air with a knife?

What about the novelist who's already worried about having to do book signings and appearances because she dreads public speaking? Or the budding freelance writer who's scared to death that he might actually get an assignment and have to write the darn thing?

I went through this the first time I got an assignment that required conducting interviews. I was afraid of cold-calling strangers, so I chose to only query for subjects I could write about without interviewing anyone other than my friends. My first published articles were profiles of my old college pals who ran successful businesses. But I feared stepping away from my safety zone. I was afraid I might actually have to speak with someone I (gasp) didn't know.

Of course, to be a successful freelance writer, I was going to have to learn to overcome this fear. It was inevitable that I'd eventually hit a subject my friends weren't experts on.

To get through it, I had to teach myself that most people love to be interviewed. Most people want to be thought of as experts in their particular arenas, and just the fact that you're calling on them is the grandest compliment, second only to "Have you lost weight?" Plus, you're offering them free publicity and a chance to express themselves to the masses. Even doctors have mothers, and those mothers just eat up the chance to show their bridge partners that their son is so well-respected that he's being quoted in a magazine.

Why Do You Fear Success?

Don't attach unnecessary stipulations on your writing career. No, you don't have to move to L.A. to be a screenwriter (though you'll probably have to visit). No, you don't have to do book signings and appearances if it makes you uncomfortable (though your mom may trick you into having one—at her house). Don't let these excuses hold you back any longer. Concentrate on today and let tomorrow take care of itself.

Sure, there are some unavoidables (like my need to do interviews to be a successful freelance writer). Tackle them head-on. Ask yourself why you're avoiding success—why you might be stymieing your own good fortune. Categorize your answers into two columns: legitimate fears and bogus excuses.

Legitimate fears might include your fear of not being able to meet a deadline, fear of bad reviews, or fear of outshining your spouse. Now ask yourself which of these things you can control, and which must be left to fate.

You can prove to yourself that you can handle deadlines without having a trial by fire. Test yourself. Set your own deadline and meet it before you start pitching your work to editors. Gain that piece of confidence.

Bad reviews and bad reviewers are out of your control, so there's no point in fearing them. Go ahead and fear them anyway if you must, but realize that this fact is never going to change—so you can either get your work out there anyway and deal with the reviews when they come, or you can hide your work away forever and avoid dealing with them. It's that simple. Which choice will you make? (Hint: the answer is, "Get my work out there.")

Outshining your spouse is only partly within your control. Yes, you might become the little star of the household, or, if you're particularly successful, a medium-sized constellation. Will that be so bad? Why would your success annoy your loved one? Give him or her a little more credit; until proven otherwise, assume that your significant other will love basking in your limelight. Just vow not to get a really swelled head when you hit the *New York Times* best-seller list, and make a point of making a big deal of your partner's successes too. And *always* mention them in your dedications. See mine for an example.

By far, the largest cause for fear of success is the fear of higher expectations. You fear that if you produce one good work, people will expect you to keep producing high-quality work. Now ask yourself this: why would you produce anything less anyway? Of course you're going to produce high-quality work. You're you, and you're a perfectionist. There's no reason to worry that after publication, all of a sudden, your talent is going to run away from home. It'll still be there for works two, three, and fifty-four, drinking your beer and taking up space on your couch.

Whatever conditions you have attached to success, unattach them. Make it worth it to succeed. Know that you can handle anything that comes your way. You've handled everything in your life thus far; certainly you can handle writing success.

▶ PROMPT: Write about something—other than a house—that's haunted.

Rejection Reflection

Every writer's work gets rejected. We've already established that depressing fact of the writing life. But what can you do with those rejections to cure your stagnation due to writer's block? Why not try something novel—and write the editor back?

This is a simple exercise that is downright guaranteed to get your blood pumping and might start your writing juices flowing.

Start by going to that "rejection place." No, I don't mean high school. You know the one. It could be a file folder, a file cabinet, a tickler file, a coupon book, a shoebox, an entire closet, or even a steel spike upon which you've sacrificed several years' worth of rejection letters by piercing them through their desiccated hearts. The spike might have some blood on the tip from the last time you missed. Wherever your own personal rejection place may be, go there. Now begin reading, one by one, your favorite or most despised rejection letters.

Don't fear them; savor them. Don't cringe; cry out—in revenge! Eye the fancy logos. Finger the fine stationary. Lick your finger and test the signature to see if it was personal or just a stamp. Whatever you do, don't let them get hold of your own personal fear factor and grab on for dear life.

Instead, think of them as someone *else*'s rejection letters; a stranger's perhaps. Or even a famous writer you've come to love and admire. You'll have a lot more fun that way (sadistic, aren't you?), and the experience won't be quite as painful.

Many of these rejections will be uninspired form letters; some will even be written in the margins. That's okay. Sometimes, those work the best. Now take out a sheet of paper and a pen, or get comfortable behind your computer, and reply. Reject the editor's rejection letter.

This is something we've been taught not to do for many, many years. "Don't *ever* respond to a negative rejection letter." So says the current—and former—wisdom. And to be fair, the current and former wisdom is rather wise. If I'd fired off a nasty letter, fax, or e-mail to every editor who'd ever rejected my work, I'd have burned too many bridges to count by now.

But no one ever said anything about simply writing a reply to a rejection letter. Did they? Well, they may have, actually, but what they meant is that you do not *mail off* a reply to a rejection letter. And that's fair. The only place you're likely to mail these replies is *Mad Magazine*, anyway.

So let's get started. Begin your rejection letter reply with a simple "Dear Sir or Madam," or, better yet, something snide such as, "To Whom It May Concern in the Department of Broken Dreams,

Trampled-on Promises, Crushed Hopes, and Daggers in the Back." Or simply, "Hey, Scumbag." (Pete Barnstrom says, "Mine usually begin, 'Dear Coprophilic Son of a Leprous Mule.'")

Take your time. After all, this is therapy and like all good therapy may take some time. Don't see it as a chore or an exercise; just enjoy it. Think of it as going back to your old elementary school and beating up the school bully (he might still be there). Think of it as telling your last boss what you really thought of her. Or how about your latest ex? *Now* you're talking!

Be nasty. Be personal. Be derogatory. Be free. Be mean, evil, wicked, and hateful. Be anything but professional. Take every rule you ever learned about professional letter writing and toss it out the window, along with your dog-eared copies of *Dealing with Editors, Handling Rejection, 101 Ways to Be Mature,* and, most important, *Writer's Etiquette.*

Let your emotions run rampant. Let your imagination go crazy. Let your inner troublemaker roam wild. Make a verbal voodoo doll by wishing famine, pestilence, and unsightly zits upon said editor.

Tap into your inner Hannibal Lecter and really let the emotions pour out onto the page. Take every rejection you've ever gotten, be it at the senior prom or trying out for the high school drama class, and focus all of the resultant anger all on that one unnamed editor at that impressive, plastic, shallow New York publisher—the same one who you're quite sure wouldn't know a good book if it bit him on the nose, but you'd sure like him to find out.

Really let him have it and, when you're done, *read* it. Enjoy it. Savor it. Smile at your candor, admire how many words you found that rhyme with "entrails," marvel at how many times you found a way to use "pedantic" in one sentence.

Sigh with satisfaction, then get back to work.

Change Your Brain

9

The Power of Thought

Lou Gehrig found out he had a fatal illness and said, "I consider myself the luckiest man on the face of the earth." How's that for an amazing perspective?

If you want to see the world differently, you *can* change the way your brain works. But today, we're not out to conquer the whole world, so we don't have to get you to change your entire outlook. Just how you see your writing.

I want you to take away the manacles. I want you to stop allowing writing to feel like a chore and instead, retrain your mind to think of writing as a reward in itself.

In his book *Break Writer's Block Now!*, Jerrold Mundis introduces something he calls the "Short-Time Method." According to this method, when you feel you're running out of steam and writer's block is heading your way, immediately cut down your writing time by at least 75 percent. In other words, if you normally write for eight hours a day, now only allow yourself to write for two.

Mundis works it out over the course of four to six weeks—the first week, he allows himself to work for only up to an hour a day; the second week, an hour and a half; the third week, no more than two hours, and so on.

Why does this work?

It's all summed up in that one simple word: "allow."

▶ PROMPT: What's the most out-of-character thing you or your character has ever done? Write about it.

Allow Yourself to Write

I'm asking you to take a big leap with me and find yourself a real "aha" moment. I want you to think about this concept: you do not *have* to write today. You are *allowing* yourself to write today. When the ice-cream man came to your neighborhood, you used to run inside and holler at the top of your lungs, "Ice-cream man is here! Mommm, can I have an ice cream?" Mom would choose whether or not to allow you to have ice cream. If you got it, it was a treat, unless it turned out to be rhubarb flavored. But there were plenty of times when mom didn't allow you to have things, too—like when you walked down the aisles of the toy store calling out, "Can we get this? How about this? This? Mom? Where are you?"

You don't need Mom's approval anymore. Now it's all up to you to decide when and how to dole out your rewards. You don't always have to allow yourself to write. You can take away that indulgence when there are more pressing things to attend to. But when you do sit down to write, tell yourself that you are giving yourself permission to write, and perhaps just for a specified period of time.

Allow Yourself to Stop

It may be hard to set boundaries with yourself, especially if you're a full-time writer or if you don't work outside the home. I still have trouble with it. With amazing regularity, you will find me with buttocks planted firmly in computer chair, typing away into the wee hours of the night (it's 5:20 A.M. right now). But that's 'cause I'm on a roll (which gives whole new meaning to "sitting on my buns"). Oh, was that rubbing it in? Well, yank my hair and call me Shirley.

It's easy to keep working until you're running on fumes. When no one's standing over you telling you to punch out, you have to count on your inner alarm clock to let you know it's quitting time. And sometimes, our inner alarm clocks get broken or beep much too quietly in the background for hours on end while we successfully tune out to its signals. So we sit there for hours longer than we should, just cranking those brain cells, trying to squeeze out one more drop of genius.

There's a point at which it becomes counterproductive to keep working. When your eyes are bloodshot, your brain is melting, and you've been metaphorically whacking away at piñatas only to find all of them devoid of any candy, it means you've taken too many liberties with your writing schedule. Cut back. Tell yourself that you will only give yourself permission to write for a specified period of time. No matter what happens, stop yourself at the end of it.

That's how you can stoke the fires again. That's how your passion can reignite and your drive can build up. Hopefully, within a day or two, you'll *want* to continue beyond your time allowance—but don't let yourself! Even if your fingers are flying and you're in the middle of writing the most brilliant thing you've ever written, avoid the possibility of writer's block coming back and play hard to get this time. Only let yourself hold hands on the first date. Then maybe a kiss on the second date. And maybe some heavy kissing on the third date. And . . . hey now, this is a PG-13-rated book.

Oh, screw it. What I'm saying here is that sitting by that computer for eight hours a day every day, trying to make words appear by sheer will, is sort of like only being satisfied with sex that results in multiple orgasms in the same way every day. Sometimes you just want a quickie. Sometimes you just want to hold hands again. Even if you do manage those multiples, they will become far less exciting and inspiring if you turn them into work by insisting that they happen all the time, no matter how long it takes or how much effort you have to put in to get there.

No, dole out those luxurious times when they happen naturally, and when you can fully enjoy them. Otherwise, tease yourself. Cutting back the time you let yourself write makes it feel more like foreplay, so you can't wait to get back to it the next day and play some more. And the good news? Computers hardly ever get headaches.

All Writing Counts

Now I want you to change your definition of writing. Who says "real" writing has to be a finished product? Who says it has to fit neatly into an established and acceptable format, like an article for a big-name magazine, a poem, or a book? I write the world's most clever to-do lists, and my fiancé is the proud recipient of hundreds of creative love letters. Does that count? You bet it does.

I don't know about you, but I've saved all of his letters to me—including the e-mails we exchanged before we even met in person—and they are among my most cherished possessions. Taking the time to write a truly heartfelt, funny, or day-brightening letter can make all the difference in the world in a relationship, romantic or otherwise.

I've also taken to writing letters to businesses lately. I wrote the GoodNites company to tell them how very much I hated their commercial with the little boy who wets the bed and has the same upward-lilting voice inflection in every line he speaks. Like, everything he says? Is a question? And it's annoying? (Yes, I got a response, and I haven't seen that commercial on the air since about two weeks after I wrote the letter. I like to think that's not a coincidence. Oh, the power of my lethal pen! Muahahaha!) Conversely, I wrote to the Serta people to tell them how very much I loved their "counting sheep" commercials. They're still on the air. I like to credit myself with that, too. Also, I invented the Internet, even before Al Gore. For that matter, I invented Al Gore.

Point is, I spent some time composing both my letters so the people on the other end would want to share them with their bosses. Any form of writing you do helps you keep that brain limber and helps you make an easier transition into writing mode whenever you want to. When you're blocked, consider getting back into the swing of things by simply communicating with people in writing again.

▶ PROMPT: If you could have one talent that you don't have now, what would it be and why?

Get the Message (Boards)

Along those lines, finding and participating in an on-line message board can be one quick way of conquering your writer's block. Go ahead, get on-line and type "message boards" into your favorite search engine. Add "writer" if you want, or perhaps your genre, such as "romance," "horror," or "mystery." Or maybe you'd prefer to take what you get—a message board for gardeners, stock-car race fans, or ship-in-a-bottle crafters.

The point is to find a message board, check it out, select one, and then start "talking."

It's just like "real" writing, only different. Whether it's debating the different kinds of model glue for putting all those ships in all those bottles, or answering a newbie writer's question at a message board for freelance writers, allow yourself to spill your guts. Let it all hang out. The nice thing is that you'll never see any of these people again.

The trick to outwitting writer's block may just be to *trick* it! Perhaps your writer's block is a snob and only considers the pieces you deem worthy enough to print out to be real, actual writing. Maybe your writer's block takes a siesta when it sees you typing in a hasty reply to some gardening, scrapbooking, or writing question.

And in taking that siesta, perhaps it leaves you alone just long enough to get your confidence back, to regain your composure and your footing, to let you feel the joy in simple, casual writing, and perhaps even recognize your natural flair for the written word.

If that's the case, then participating in a few targeted message boards might just be the first, tentative baby step back to your real writing. If so, your writer's block will soon be getting "the message."

You Have Boundless Creativity

"We must learn to trust that creativity is indeed endless, inexhaustible, and easily accessible, once we learn work habits that keep us from getting in its way," says Susan Shaw, certified hypnotherapist.

It may seem that we've used up all of our ideas. This feeds into the fallacy that our idea well is finite. Just as people originally thought the world was flat, so do we sometimes falsely believe our brains only have a certain quota of good ideas and after it's reached, we're sunk. When we're blocked, it can feel like our brains are as blank as a new blackboard, but in reality we have about 72,000 thoughts a day. Every day. You just can't stop those suckers from coming—much like door-to-door salesmen.

Out of those 72,000 thoughts, surely one or two are worthy of writing down. Don't buy into the pessimistic thought that you've run out of things to write about. Instead, learn to listen to yourself—really listen. More than likely, when you think you've run out of ideas, the truth is that you've simply discounted them. An idea flashes by in a millisecond, and by your next heartbeat you've already decided it's a stupid, unworthy, or unmarketable idea.

The truth is that in its original, most simple incarnation, that may be true. Maybe you get a flash of an idea about a man who dies and wants to communicate with his wife to give her one last message ("Could you water the plants?"). In the next instant, you think: *Ghost.* It's already been done. Forget it.

But hear yourself out. If you give yourself a minute to stew about it, you might find that you have a brand new spin on this idea. Maybe his message isn't a simple "I love you." Maybe he wants to tell her the truth about a crime he committed, so she can help free the man who's serving time in his place. Or that he has a great deal of money hidden somewhere. Or maybe, rather than appearing by possessing the body of a psychic, he comes to her in dreams, or is reborn as the next-door neighbor's dog, or . . .

You *do* have ideas. Plenty of them. Going back to our discussion in chapter 5, you must simply allow your mind some time to roam without boundaries. Give it the quiet it deserves so it can speak to you. Don't keep scolding it like a chattering child in a church. You must respect your creativity enough to encourage its growth. Recognize that not all ideas will come out fully formed and bullet proof straight from the womb of your brain, but instead will need some coaxing, nurturing, and development. Give them this time, and learn to acknowledge and appreciate all of your creative thoughts, the winners and the losers alike.

As written in *A Course in Miracles*, "You can wait, delay, paralyze yourself, or reduce your creativity almost to nothing. But you cannot abolish it. You can destroy your medium of communication, but not your potential."

10

Ohmmmm, Ohmmmm: Dealing with the Stress of Writer's Block

Writer's block is stressful. From worrying about when you'll get the magic back to stressing over an upcoming deadline, one bad block can send your stress level skyrocketing. Sometimes, the best thing you can do for yourself is to take some time away from the writing and try some relaxation techniques to get yourself back to a state of peace and calm.

Try these techniques:

• **Belly breathing.** Did you know that most people don't know how to breathe effectively? You'd think that would be instinctive, but no. Most people take shallow breaths from their chests rather than taking full breaths from their diaphragms. To calm yourself down quickly, take slow, deep breaths from the gut. To practice doing this, lie flat on your back with a book on your stomach. When you inhale, try to make the book rise, and not your chest. Inhale to the count of five, exhale to the count of ten. Repeat this until your pulse rate slows down and you feel more relaxed. Then make fun of all the unenlightened people ("You don't even know how to breathe correctly!").

• **Go herbal.** Certain herbs and essential oils are great for relaxation. Lavender can be used on the body (put a few drops of lavender oil on pressure points—wrists, temples, neck, back of knees), in a bath, or sprayed on linens (for all you bachelors, that's sheets and stuff). In the summertime, I've been known to put a few drops of lavender oil on tissues and then stick them in the air-conditioning vent. It disseminates the scent around the room wonderfully. Also, try chamomile tea. But you should drink it, not pour it into the air-conditioning vent.

• **"I'm good enough, I'm smart enough . . ."** Take a tip from Stuart Smalley and use affirmations to your benefit. Affirmations are positive messages that you repeat to yourself to achieve better physical, mental, and spiritual health, and they can really help to build up your confidence and unblock you. Come up with a few catch phrases like "I am a talented writer" and "My writing is meaningful and makes a difference in the world" and "This ransom note is so good, they'll never know it's from me." Keep your affirmations in the present tense (not "I will be a talented writer") to recognize that you already are capable and ready, not that you will be some faraway day. Speak your affirmations out loud (well, maybe not the bit about the ransom note), record them on a tape and listen to them, or write them down several times a day. If you want to learn more about affirmations, visit www.poweraffirmations.com. You'll find a free five-minute audio sample at www.poweraffirmations.com/sample.wav and several pages of sample Power Affirmations.

• **Work it, baby.** I don't really need to tell you about the benefits of exercise, do I? That's like telling you that smoking is bad for your health. (Although that doesn't stop people from telling me so—all the time. I like to respond, "*Really*?! And here I thought it was prolonging my life!" I wonder how they'd feel if I started rolling my own and filling them with chamomile tea.) As well as helping all your body parts work better and making you look hot in a bathing suit, exercise also releases endorphins in your brain, which puts you in a better mood and helps you think more clearly. Make it a point to exercise at least three times a week, preferably before you sit down to write (or in the middle, if you need a pick-me-up). Start today. Not tomorrow. Today.

• **Be progressive.** Progressive muscle relaxation is a terrific way to unwind, even if you only have a few minutes free. Here's how it works: lie down on your back and make a fist with your right hand. Hold for five seconds, then release. Repeat with your left hand. Then tense your right upper arm. Hold for five seconds, then release. Repeat with your left arm. Follow this tense-and-release exercise with these remaining body parts in this order: lower legs; upper legs; eye muscles, forehead, and scalp; cheeks; mouth; neck, chest, abdomen, back; buttocks and pelvic floor. At the end, your whole body will feel looser, and you'll be ready for another round at the computer—just as soon as you manage to get up again. To learn more about progressive relaxation, you may be interested in the book *Anger and Anxiety* by Dr. Bob Rich (http://users.tpg.com.au/bobr/psych//stress1.html).

• **Meditate.** Meditation doesn't have to be all New-Agey. It can be, if you want, but it doesn't have to be. It is a way of focusing your attention to help you achieve a higher level of consciousness. It can promote healing, lower your blood pressure, increase your creativity, and help you deal with stress. An easy way to begin meditating is to sit down in a comfortable position, concentrate on a fixed object a few feet away from you (candles are popular), and repeat a one-word mantra (like "peace," "relax," or "breathe") in your mind over and over. Mantras can also be words like "ohm" or "hamsa," used just to help you focus inward.

When your mind wanders to outside thoughts, or sounds interfere, just acknowledge them and allow them to pass through. Keep coming back to the mantra and to slow, steady breaths. To learn more about meditation, visit the Worldwide Online

Meditation Center at www.meditationcenter.com or Meditation and Alternative Medicine at www.alternative-medicine.net.

You can also try guided meditations. There are many recordings available, but I have a particular fondness for the Brain Sync spirituality series (www.brainsync.com). This is a highly researched program that uses precisely tuned sound waves at different frequencies to help you achieve your desired mental state (alertness/concentration, visualization/creativity, meditation/intuition, or healing/sleep). The soothing voice on the recordings talks you through several relaxing "scenes." Though I still can't explain exactly why, I felt such a profound sense of release while listening to one of the tapes that I cried. And I'm no weepy sissy, either. Try a free ten-minute "brain tune-up" at www.brainsync.com/relaxnow.asp.

• **"Calgon, take me away!"** This may seem like a no-brainer, but ask yourself: When was the last time you took a nice, long, good, hot bubble bath? Last week? Last month? Last year? Last *decade*? In any case, it's just not enough. For starters, you stink to high heaven. Baths are one of the cheapest, easiest, not to mention cleanest forms of relaxation available to modern-day writers, unless you share an apartment with a bunch of guys, in which case, it would be healthier to swim in toxic waste. Sometimes, just the thought of a hot bath is enough to relax me. And even better, by the time I'm through selecting my latest bath product du jour at the local Bath & Body Works, or a cheap variation thereof at Dollar Works, I'm nearly in a coma! My fiancé's always carrying me home over his shoulder.

The very names of today's bath products alone are designed to relax: Soothing Mist. Sensual Sea Foam. Luscious Lavender. Peaceful Peach. Aromatic Apple. Coma Coconut. And whether your bubbles of choice are bath beads, scented oils, fresh flowers, crystal salts, or good old Mr. Bubble (I don't want to know the other way you make bubbles in there), the combination of that hot, steamy water and those rich, fragrant bubbles is enough to make any writer's troubles sink to the bottom of the tub—and then keep right on going down the drain.

But baths don't have to wait for nightfall. Start your day off with a bath instead of a shower. Bring your coffee in with you and let the warm water and sweet caffeine turn your frown upside down. Or make it a lunchtime tradition to cool off with a little sweet iced tea and hot, soapy lather in a noon-day bath. The combinations of food, bubbles, and time are endless—and so are the relaxing benefits of a nice, hot bubble bath.

• **Repeat after me.** Repetitive activities are also great to help you relax and free up your mind to wrap itself around stunning new writing ideas. Knitting, crocheting, doing the dishes, telling your kids to go to bed, and working in a vitamin factory all qualify, though I don't recommend that last one. I worked in a vitamin factory where my sole responsibility was to stick a coupon into every bottle that came down the line for eight hours a day—ten if I did overtime. Now do you pity me?

It's also well documented that petting an animal slows your heart rate and helps you to simmer down. I've tried this with my pet fish with disastrous results. You may have more luck with your furry creatures. Writer and editor Christine R. McLaughlin likes to pet her golden retriever when she's in a funk. "Something about petting that furry head and kissing it helps me rejuvenate and refocus."

▶ PROMPT: Describe your character from several people's points of view. How would her mother describe her? How about her ex-boyfriend? Her best friend? Her neighbor?

Using Music to Relax

Two popular forms of relaxation techniques can be found as close as your radio, stereo, or bedroom boombox. For starters, try investing in a few of those nature recordings that are so popular these days. I often find such CDs to be less than five dollars at the local Best Buy or Circuit City, and they come in all tastes and preferences. For those who find Celtic music relaxing, you can find tapes mixing traditional Celtic classics with the sounds of whales, or rain, or rushing rapids.

There are relaxation CDs mixing Christmas carols with the howls of wolves (nothing like the threat of being eaten by wolves to bring a family closer together at Christmastime), and lilting piano with the evocative cry of whales at sea. The combinations are endless and proliferate in the New Age section of your local record or department store. From lions in the Serengeti to Native American drums, the choices for relaxation are as endless as your needs to relax.

I find that these CDs are best enjoyed at a low volume, usually only three or four on my stereo (which goes to eleven). Dimming the lights helps, too, and a candle never hurts. Then I recline on the couch, or sometimes even the floor, watching the candlelight flicker on the ceiling and listening to the strains of my relaxing New Age CD. In minutes, my eyes are closed and no matter how many dishes are in the sink or pages are left to do before my deadline, I am instantly transported to a far distant world, be it Africa, Ireland, or some exotic locale found only in my imagination, like Three-Dollar-a-Word-Land. Regardless, in five to fifteen minutes the tension has left my body for the rest of the evening, and I am free to either return to my writing, or chill out in any way I see fit.

The second relaxation technique involving a CD player is a little more energetic, yet just as freeing: dance! Yes, I know I already covered exercise, but dancing is so much more than jumping rope or lifting weights. It doesn't matter if you're married, recently divorced, attached, or stubbornly single. You don't need a partner to dance these days, especially if you're employing this relaxation technique with a CD containing your favorite dance tracks from the '80s, the '90s, or even today. (In fact, it might be better if you're dancing solo!)

I am the proud owner of several cheesy disco CDs featuring the likes of Donna Summer, The Village People, and Regina Bell, also found in the bargain bins at today's bigger electronics stores. As soon as the opening strains of "You Can Ring My Be-e-ell" leave the stereo speakers, I am off and running on a dancing jag that can last the length of the CD. (Just be sure you don't put it on "repeat" or you'll die of exhaustion.)

Naturally, I close the windows, draw the drapes, and bar the door, but once I'm in my own little world and know that no one can see me, off I go to the disco heydays of my writer's-block-free youth. The physical activity of moving your arms and legs, swiveling your thighs, and shaking your hips, combined with the bubblegum music of yesteryear is an irresistible cocktail for mood-altering relaxation. Before the second song, you're bound to forget where you are, who you are, and what you were so stressed about a mere seven minutes ago. Disco may be dead, but that only makes the CDs all the cheaper for this great relaxation technique.

Invent Your Own Relaxation Technique

Of course, you can also experiment with your own relaxation techniques. "Sometimes, if I'm really feeling hopeless, I just lie flat on my back on the carpet for at least five minutes, counting seconds by the tick of my wall clock," says Sabina C. Becker. "This simmers me down to a comfortable level; I can't dwell on

how bad a writer I am if I'm busy counting five times sixty ticks.
I hate to lose count!"

Just don't get *too* relaxed. There are still quite a few chapters
to go.

*Every time I've had writer's block, it resulted from a barrage of
rejections for the book that I naïvely thought would be "the
one." I sometimes get an overwhelming feeling of failure and
dread when the rejections pile up. The first one's not so bad, the
second one makes it a little worse, then by the fifth or sixth, it's
like all of New York is laughing at me in some satirical weekly
column by Candace Bushnell. Then I make the mistake of
wandering through a bookstore to "cheer myself up" and see
three books just like mine—and I mean, call-the-lawyers-this-
can't-be-a-coincidence-just-like-mine—blazing a path up the
best-seller list. Those are the times I decide to chuck it all and
give up for a while.*

*I try to use my blocks to my advantage, though. I relax by
reading several true crime books and don't think about my
writing career at all. I eat too much, sleep too much, and it goes
on like that for a few days. Then one day, I wake up recharged,
sell my true crimes back to the bookstore, and plug myself back
into the computer with a brand new "I'll show them" attitude.
Might not work for everybody, but it works for me.*

—Rusty Fischer, author of *Beyond the Bookstore: 101
(Other) Places to Sell Your Self-Published Book*

11

O Deadline, My Deadline

Break Down Your Writing into Small Pieces

Deadlines can be the cause or the cure of the dreaded block. For those who freeze up when a deadline is looming, learn to break down your writing into small, manageable chunks. It's sort of like that old saying, "inch by inch, life's a cinch." Of course, when you're blocked, nothing seems like a cinch, but you see where I'm going.

If you've got to hit 500 words a day, do 250 words in the morning and 250 at night. If you get behind, as we invariably do, and your word count doubles up, split it up into chunks of 333 words, three times a day. It's easy for me to say "don't procrastinate and leave everything for the last minute," but it may be hard to break that kind of habit.

Nevertheless, I'm going to say it anyway: don't procrastinate and leave everything for the last minute! When you get a deadline, your very first thought should be to create a plan of attack. It may look something like this:

Article due Monday, May 27

Monday, May 13: Begin research on-line. Locate experts and send them e-mails or make phone calls to arrange interviews.

Tuesday, May 14: Conduct research at library.
Thursday, May 16: Conduct interviews.
Saturday, May 18: Write lead and first half of rough draft.
Monday, May 20: Write second half of rough draft.
Friday, May 24: Edit and revise.
Saturday, May 25: Proofread and turn in assignment.

Did you notice I turned in the assignment two days early? Always plan for that. Plan to turn in all short assignments (articles, short stories, etc.) at least two days early, and long assignments (books, term papers, etc.) a full week early. This gives you built-in emergency time in case you get sick, have an interviewee cancel, or have an off day when you just can't stand looking at your computer. (Don't worry—if you're still in your pajamas and haven't had a shower yet, it probably can't stand looking at you, either.)

It's also a good idea to prepare to be *un*prepared. By that, I mean never plan everything out to the day even if you're leaving in a two-day short article stopgap and a week-long book stopgap. Notice how there are some days not accounted for in the example above? Those are built-in days for flexibility, emergencies, or callbacks. Those are built-in places where I'm preparing to be unprepared.

For instance, what if an interviewee can't talk to you on the day you scheduled it? (Doesn't this yahoo know you've got a deadline?!) Well, since you've prepared to be unprepared, you shift the interview to another day. Or, if the interviewee can't talk at all (too busy, laryngitis, became a mime artist, etc.), you have time to find someone else. You don't abandon your schedule, you just rework it.

Naturally, there are times when you take a last-minute assignment for various reasons—an editor you've always wanted to work with, a publication that would be a jewel in your résumé, a big, huge, glorious, fat paycheck—that don't give you a whole lot of leeway. In such cases, you have to work on it every single day. But in most cases, you'll have a reasonable amount of time to work.

▶ PROMPT: A man has died. His worst nightmare has come true: now his family will go through his house and discover his deepest secret. What is it? How will his family discover it?

Padding Your Schedule

Another good tactic for de-stressing yourself when you face a looming deadline is learning how to pad your schedule by pushing ahead on the days when the writing is really flowing. So what if you're only scheduled to write 500 words today? If the juices are flowing and those first 500 come almost effortlessly, push forward with another 500. Or 400. Or 250. Whatever. When you're hot, you're hot! You wouldn't abandon a slot machine that kept spitting out quarters, would you? And your cat can learn how to use a can opener. Just don't fall into the trap of writing until you're exhausted and bone dry. Quit while you still have some writing energy left.

Padding your schedule is another instance of preparing to be unprepared. After all, for every day when the juices are sizzling hot and we can crank out 1,000 words without a problem, there are just as many days—if not twice as many—where it's a strain and a struggle to get down 50 words, let alone 500.

But it's not just your word count you need to pad. Need to conduct an interview for a story that's due? How many questions are you going to ask? If you think you need to ask eight, ask ten. Always ask an extra question or two just in case the answers you get don't quite match up to your expectations. Nothing kills a deadline like lack of information, and while you can pad the word count of your questions all you like, you can't make up an interviewee's answers for them (darn it!). Once they've spoken with you, it's often next to impossible to do it all over again just because you didn't ask enough—or good enough—questions the first time around.

Your research should be padded as well. If consulting four books is a good idea, consulting six books is an even better one. Even if you don't consult six books, write down the titles of the two or three you don't use, just in case one of your original picks turns out to be written by the same people who translated your VCR manual from Japanese to English. (I hate those people!)

Respect Your Limits

The discipline required to keep to a deadline is one of the most important skills a writer can have. Know your limits and never drive when you're over them. Also, never agree to a deadline you know you can't keep. I know it's tempting. As writers, we tend to be a needy lot. Perhaps not emotionally needy, but often *financially* needy.

We know that when it's dry, it's desert dry, and when it rains, it pours, turning that desert into mud, which your husband then spreads all through the house with his boots, despite the fact you've told him to take them off at the front door a thousand times and . . . sorry. Where was I? Oh, yeah—we need the money (probably to get the carpets cleaned again). And as such, we often find it hard to turn down writing jobs, whether they come during a drought or a flood. And with a desperate editor on the line, offering you all kinds of incentives if you meet this "unmeetable" deadline, it can be tempting to acquiesce.

As hard as it may seem at times, try to avoid this editorial trap. It's just not worth it. Unless you're particularly good at turning water into wine, you probably can't add extra hours to your day, either. Be honest and tell the editor you have too much on your plate to meet such a short deadline. If you don't tell her and you don't meet the deadline, you'll put an editor in a terrible position, and she'll never hire you again. Once you get a deadline, consider it binding. If you encounter serious problems along the way (can't find anyone to interview, your research isn't pulling up current statistics, etc.) let the editor know early in the process. She may be able to help you, or she may extend your deadline—but only if you give her enough notice to alter her schedule.

Editors are to writers what bosses are to the rest of the world, and no one ever wants to tick off the boss. But what would make an editor angrier: knowing that a writer was going to miss her deadline and thus having the time to make alternative arrangements, or the writer simply missing the deadline without making a peep and forcing the editor to scramble to find something else to run? Trust me, tell your editor. If you're lucky, she built some padding into her schedule as well, and can offer you a little leeway.

Create Self-imposed Deadlines

But what if you're not working on assignment? There are many pros and cons of deadlines, but for those of us prone to procrastination, they can be a true blessing in disguise. At least with a firm deadline, there is a demarcation point—a line in the sand, a big red date looming in huge numbers on your calendar.

Without a deadline, a writer is left to his or her own devices and the opportunity for writer's block to rear its ugly head is riper than a three-month-old banana.

If you have trouble motivating yourself, it can be very helpful to create self-imposed deadlines, building yourself a whole lot of cushion time. Interviewees can have weeks to respond instead of days. And now you can afford to wait on those interlibrary loans from the good library downtown instead of using the tiny reference section at the cruddy little annex next to your apartment complex. You can also be more flexible with your daily, weekly, or even monthly word counts.

Just pretend you're on assignment and create that same kind of day-by-day schedule. Don't let the fact that you're not on a real deadline allow you to lapse into some kind of trancelike lull where you simply key in a few sentences every morning and then spend the rest of the day stalking your favorite soap opera stars.

I recommend getting on a sliding-scale deadline. In other words, find some kind of way to reward yourself for *beating* your self-imposed deadline. A night out on the town, a day with that best-seller you've been meaning to get to, a weekend getaway, a new printer. Whatever. This way, when the writing *is* going well, the juices are flowing, and the pages are adding up (or if they're really clever, doing long division), you won't be tempted to slack off just because you're ahead of schedule. Instead, you'll have a personal incentive of your own choosing to urge you on, keep you going, and make headway on your own deadline—or even surpass it.

If self-imposed deadlines are still a little too lenient for you, why not pretend? Pretend that book is anxiously awaited at a big New York publishing house. Pretend your favorite author is eagerly waiting for the rough draft so he can give you a great promotional blurb for the back cover. You can even ask someone to play the role of editor—tell a writing friend that you're going to turn in this piece on a certain date, and tell him to make you stick to it. He doesn't have to offer feedback if you don't want him to, but send it to him nonetheless, just so you'll have a sense of responsibility and closure.

You can return the favor, and perhaps even aid in your own recovery from writer's block, by offering to edit one of your friend's pieces. Often, reading someone else's work, objectively and with brand new eyes (which you bought just for the occasion), can help you improve not only his story, but your own as well. You will undoubtedly learn from your friend's mistakes; you'll learn to spot overwritten dialogue, poor transitions, weak openings, and many other potential problems. Likewise, you can learn to analyze what works and why, and apply that to your writing.

▶ PROMPT: Write a short story using only words of no less than three letters. That means you can't use the words "to," "a," "at," "I," "go," and the like.

Find a Deadline Buddy

It can also help to have a self-imposed-deadline buddy. If you're finding it hard to stick to your self-imposed deadline and your friend is being a little too friendly in letting you slide on those progressive word counts, find somebody who is writing an article, paper, or book around the same length as yours, which is "due" at about the same time, and buddy up on checking in with each other throughout the process.

You can work together on a reasonable deadline, have checkpoints along the way, and even critique sessions where you share your writing up to a certain point and get—and give—valuable feedback on the work that's been produced so far.

Enter Quickie Contests

There are also several contests that exist just for the purpose of making writers work quickly. Check out these:

Anvil Press 3-Day Novel Contest (www.anvilpress.com/3daynov/index.htm). This contest has been going on for twenty-five years. Sometimes called a "trial by deadline," it attracts more than 500 writers each year, and several have gone on to have their speed-written opuses published. If you're interested in playing along and don't have any plans for Labor Day weekend (or if you do and want to get out of them), you can find their guidelines on-line, or by writing to Anvil Press, #204-A 175 East Broadway, Vancouver, BC, Canada V5T 1W2. There's an entry fee (currently $35).

National Novel Writing Month (www.nanowrimo.com). If three days just sounds ridiculous, how about a month? This isn't exactly a contest; it's more of a challenge. As they put it, "It's all about quantity, not quality. The kamikaze approach forces you to lower your expectations, take risks, and write on the fly." It happens every November, and had 5,000 participants in 2001 (700 of them finished their novels on time). There's no entry fee and no prizes. It's just about motivating yourself to write 50,000 words.

The 24-hour Short Story Contest (http://www.writer-sweekly.com). Maybe novels aren't your thing. Here's a quarterly short story contest, instead. There's a small entry fee (currently $5) and lots of prizes. On the day of the contest, participants get their topic in an e-mail, and they have one day to send in their stories. It's limited to 500 writers per quarter.

Toasted Cheese "Three Cheers and a Tiger" Short Story Contest (http://www.toasted-cheese.com). The subject and length (300–2500 words) are posted at the start of this semiannual contest, and then you have forty-eight hours to write your entry. There is no entry fee, and there are small prizes for the winners.

Non-quickie Contests

Of course, there are plenty of other contests that aren't all about kamikaze writing, but can still motivate you to write according to a deadline. Pick any contest you like and just make it your mission to have your entry in before the due date.

I know lots of screenwriters who just happen to finish their new screenplays every year just days before the Nicholl Fellowships deadline. Without this contest to motivate them, it's likely that those screenplays would sit idly.

"The most effective way for me to get over writer's block is to decide to meet a deadline set by an outside force," says writer Jennifer L. Baum. "Whether it's a contest deadline, an editor's deadline, or a meeting with my script coach, needing to have something by a certain date works every time."

Many well-known writers will tell you that writing contests are a great way to break into the writing field. I'm less convinced in most contests' abilities to jump-start a career than I am convinced that they're a great training ground. Contests push you to be the best writer you can be, and they force you to adhere to guidelines and deadlines. If you're not yet confident enough to turn in your writing for publication, try entering contests first. You'll quickly find out how well you work under pressure.

If you're thinking about taking on assignments in your writing career, then enter contests where the topic is given to you, rather than free-form contests. This will show you whether or not you can work on the fly and take direction.

Submitting on a Schedule

If contests aren't your thing, or the contests I mentioned just aren't enough for your prolific self, why not try a committed campaign of submitting brand new material to new markets—on a self-imposed deadline? After all, it's not likely that an editor at *GQ* is going to take part in your healthy attempts to outwit writer's block. But there's no reason you can't include the men's fashion magazine on your road to recovery.

Start by reading their guidelines and, if possible, obtaining a sample copy and theme list. Devour this information and then choose a date by which you would like to submit a short story, feature article, designer profile, or other piece appropriate for this internationally renowned periodical. Depending on the length of the piece, set your deadline for one, two, or up to three months away. Then meet it. (Say "hi" for me.)

How good are your chances of getting published in *GQ?* Not that hot. How good are the chances that this exercise will go a long way toward breaking down your writer's block? Excellent.

Try this form of therapy with other national magazines, from *Woman's Day* to *Playboy.* Try it with smaller, more specific trade magazines, such as those catering to woodworkers, coin collectors, or model-train enthusiasts. Or you can impose a deadline for a simple letter to the editor of your local newspaper. The trick is to make a deadline, write toward that deadline, and most important, *meet* your deadline. Each time you do, your chances of beating writer's block improve, as do your chances of being published.

▶ PROMPT: "Now you've really crossed the line." Why? Write a story about someone who has crossed the line in some way.

One-Minute Deadlines

Freelancer Joe Larkin gives himself truly wacky deadlines: one minute.

On National Public Radio, Joe heard about an exercise Bobby McFerrin (of "Don't Worry, Be Happy" fame) does to stimulate his creativity: he writes one-minute pieces of music. Music critic Tom Moon explained McFerrin's "beat-the-clock" writing method: "On deadline to fulfill an opera commission, he figured the best way to create was to pressurize the writing process. His rules were simple: first thought, best thought. No stopping to evaluate the results. Once he had an idea, he'd record it, then move on."

Joe decided to try it with his poetry. "It makes you get right down to it," he says. "Can't say that what I produced was any good, but at least it made me write, and I will continue. I like the concept of pressurizing, putting yourself under the gun, but for only brief stretches, one minute at a time. One minute is easy."

I encourage you to set your own deadlines and test your limits. Give yourself just fifteen minutes to write a short story. Don't look back at what you've written—just do it. Prove to yourself that your brain can work under pressure. You may be amazed at just how coherent you can be, even when you're not stopping to think. Or you may find out you're a raving lunatic on overdrive. Need I remind you how many famous writers are actually raving lunatics?

James Robert Daniels is also a fan of working quickly. "I take short deadlines and then set a shorter target date for myself every time," he says. When he set out to write his first screenplay, he picked up *How To Write a Movie in 21 Days* by Viki King—and then he did it.

There was once a Web site called Image to Words that has, unfortunately, disappeared into the vortex of the Internet. But you can still use the exercise it offered, albeit requiring a little more legwork. At this site, writers were shown five pictures. Your objective was to type the first word that came to your head after looking at each picture, sort of like a Rorschach inkblot test. After you'd finished typing in your five words, you'd be whisked off to a clean screen, where you had five minutes to write a short story using all five words. (There was a timer to show how much time was left). If you tried the exercise again, the pictures wouldn't change, but you'd be given new instructions (for example, your words could only be interjections, like "ouch!").

If you want to try this exercise on your own, get creative: Hunt for five interesting photos on the Internet, type the first word that comes to mind for each, and set a stopwatch to give yourself five minutes to write a story incorporating those words. Here's a good spot to find thousands of photographs: http://gallery.yahoo.com. Unfortunately for me, when I look at a picture of a sunflower, the first word I think of is sunflower, so I do better with more abstract images than photos of recognizable things. If you're like that, too, try these sites: www.urban75.org/photos/abstract or www.jsalvador.com/abstracts.html (or just type "abstract images" or "abstract photographs" into your favorite search engine).

There are many writing instructors who teach the benefits of speedwriting. The object of writing in fast gear isn't to come up with work that's ready to be published; it's to give you a starting place and a sense of accomplishment. Later, you can slow down to write your second draft. Or you can keep working like a zooted-up nut with your hair on fire. Whatever works.

Work with Other Writers

If speed is not the problem, perhaps the solitary effort of writing is hanging you up. Contests, no matter what their deadline, are often just another form of writing all alone, which is not a bad thing. After all, it's not realistic or beneficial to expect never to have to write alone. But when writer's block takes center stage, all bets are off and you're free to do whatever it takes to beat it back into submission—including buddying up.

A few years ago, several talented and famous writers from Florida, including such hot and heavy hitters as Carl Hiaasen, Edna Buchanan, James W. Hall, Dave Barry, and Elmore Leonard got together and decided to write a unique and entertaining book together. The result was *Naked Came the Manatee*, a serial novel written in installments by thirteen of south Florida's hottest and most accomplished authors. Each author took a chapter, embellished on the last, often including their own creations from other novels, and concluded with a rollicking romp through Florida's literary landscape as humid and hilarious as a Jimmy Buffet album.

Why not do the same? Okay, so Dave Barry and Elmore Leonard aren't returning your calls. So what? You've got thirteen friends, don't you? Okay, how about *three*? Gee, what's wrong with you? Do you pick your nose or something? Okay, I'll settle for one—who can write, that is. In any event, tailor this elaborate writing prompt to your own personal situation and get by with a little help from your friends.

Start the book off, or finish it up. Do it by phone, by fax, or by e-mail attachments. Start with a rough outline, flesh it out to the approval of the group, and once all of you have agreed upon a page count, chapter number, and word count for each author, set to it. What a fun way to beat writer's block and get to know your fellow writers.

12

Dead Ends and Wrong Ways

The Problem with "The One"

One of the easiest ways to send yourself straight to Writer's Block Row is to tell yourself that this one is going to be your masterpiece. This is The One that's going to make up for all the junk you've ever written. This is the one that's going to be so brilliant it will make your old English teacher weep at how she misjudged your abilities. It's going to be a best-seller, and everyone is going to throw roses at your feet, and Oprah is going to send you expensive jewelry to bribe you to come on her show.

And so you sit down and can't form a single sentence that's good enough for this almighty concept. You start. You stop. You hem. You haw. You seriously contemplate clipping your toenails. Your beginning keeps getting pushed back because of the intricate backstory you just have to have to illuminate the symbolism of your great brainchild, and in the process you get farther and farther away from the ending. Before you know it your writing has gone so far back you're drawing woolly mammoths all over the page, and all your characters grunt at each other.

You trade in your ten-dollar words for twenty-dollar words, and your sentences get longer and longer—or shorter and

137

shorter. You're either so sure that the words are flowing through you exactly as they intended that you don't edit a thing, or you're so eager to get things perfect that you edit everything into oblivion.

You wake up in the middle of the night teeming with ideas, scribble them down in your handy notebook (which is starting to annoy your partner, especially when you do it during sex), and with dedication, commitment, and your two index fingers, key them into your computer the very next morning. Then, by midafternoon, they seem less like pearls of wisdom and more like smelly oyster shells. Vowing never to use the trite oyster-and-pearl simile again, you scrap the whole lot, go back to bed (or the couch, depending on how annoyed your partner is), and wake up at 3 A.M. with more late-night meanderings that don't quite cut the mustard in the harsh light of six hours later.

Your self-imposed deadline keeps getting pushed back (just like you do whenever you try to sneak back into bed) because nothing is ever good enough, and after a year and a half you're ready to scrap the whole thing and learn how to be a professional bowler because none of it, not one single word, seems worth the paper it's printed on.

So much for The One.

Now I'm not saying that you shouldn't have high hopes for your work. Of course you should. But insisting on perfection just makes you freeze up, because no words will do justice to that image you have in your head of the Perfect Masterpiece.

You can't consciously write a masterpiece. You can't know whether something is your very best piece of work until you've amassed an entire body of work over your entire writing life. Maybe your masterpiece won't happen until you're ninety ("How to Beat Senility," by . . . damn, I knew it a minute ago!). Maybe it already happened, and you just don't realize that the novel you've thrown into a drawer is sheer brilliance. But more than likely, you'll just keep getting better with time, and slowly but surely, your work will come closer and closer to your high ideals.

The problem with setting out to write the best thing you've ever written is that you become overly protective of it, and you don't let yourself take risks with it for fear of spoiling its golden sheen.

You must see every project as a work in progress. It may turn out to be glorious, or it may end up on the cutting-room floor. Don't ever get so invested in a concept that you don't allow yourself to sully it with less than perfect writing.

▶ PROMPT: When was the last time you felt put on the spot? Maybe it was when your husband asked if your mother-in-law could stay for the weekend—in front of her—or maybe it was when a potential employer caught you fudging on your résumé. Write about it.

Writers Get to Make Temporary Decisions

Every time you sit down to write, you have a choice to make. Which word will you use? The entire secret to getting rid of writer's block is to simply choose a word. And then another. And another. They may be the wrong words, they may be clunkers, they may be slugs, but each of them represents a decision. The beauty of our work is that we can always go back and change any of our decisions if they turn out to be bad ones. So you can take away the fear of making a bad choice; if you find yourself indecisive, just remind yourself that you get to rewrite history as many times as you like.

Where else in life can you do that? You can't take back your decision to get married, go to a certain college, or gamble away your earnings. You can get divorced, transfer schools, or find a nice bank that gives away toasters, but you can't erase the fact that you did all of those things in the first place. Therefore, we're conditioned to believe that our decisions are important and have consequences.

In writing, the only consequence is the passing of time (and possibly your fish, if you never clean its tank). No one ever has to see your rough drafts, so the worst thing you can lose by choosing the wrong words is time. (The fish was swimming crookedly anyway.) And if you've enjoyed the process of writing, that's no loss. It's your sweat equity, but it's time well spent.

The Value of Distance

I once found myself falling in love with one of my characters, Melanie. The simple act of describing her, of thinking about what she might say in this instance or do to that character was thrilling. As time went on, as the writing poured out of me, I wound up involving this character more and more. She hadn't appeared so prominently in my outline, that was for sure—she had started out as a minor character.

But like a ruffled old character actor in a movie who steals every scene from his better-looking, better-paid, better-billed leading man, I found this character fascinating. Intriguing. Engrossing. Adjective inducing. If I were making a movie I would have said something really original like, "The camera loves her." But as clichéd as that is, it was also very true.

She not only appeared in every scene, even scenes where she wasn't necessary, but she *took over* every scene as well—important scenes, delicate scenes that were necessary to lay the foundation for the book's surprise ending. Still, I thought she helped the flow. She took over when a scene got rough, provided a little light and air when things got too dense and heavy. Perhaps she was my muse come to life, perhaps she was just an old college friend I was subconsciously missing, whatever—she took hold of that book and led me straight through to its satisfying climax.

Then, as I do all my completed works, I set that book aside for three weeks. I was happily busy on a few other things (each depending on which channel the TV was on), and I knew that the longer I stayed away, the more distance I gave myself, the more objective I'd be when I finally returned to it. And how! When I finally picked up this 350-page opus, I was shocked— nay, embarrassed—to find that this fascinating female character had not only taken over my book, but ruined it! Hussy!

It was a miserable experience, and I felt crushed. The mere weight of this large book, and the fact that it was all but unreadable (what with the teardrops and all), sent me into a deep, dark funk as bad as any case of writer's block I'd ever had. Then, a magical thing happened. I woke up bright and early one morning (okay, that's a lie—it was probably late afternoon), ran to my word processor, poured a cup of coffee while it was booting up, and promptly saved my book into two different documents: "With HER," and "Without HER."

Only one was useful to me, of course: "Without HER." And, as I spent a solid week slicing this ethereal character out of my novel, I began to see its potential. There was more work to do, of course. I had to replace an overblown character with one who was less obvious, but the book not only got shorter in the process, it got better.

And when I'm ready to write a story about a strong female lead, I've already got one. So you see, sometimes sentences, paragraphs, whole scenes, and, occasionally entire books occasionally write themselves. Obviously, I was choosing the words as I wrote them. But once I got started, I simply couldn't stop. And when I did, after just a little distance, I was able to save one book, and set aside half of another.

Such is the beauty of writing, of time, and of objective distance.

Until the moment your work is accepted by a publisher, you have the ability to erase every single decision you made. Chances are, some of them were good ones, even if others aren't working for you. With each draft, you'll get a little closer to what you really want to say.

Enjoy Each Stage

Think of your work as having many layers. Not like an onion, which smells bad. But more like the human body, which is beautiful. You start with the very, very rough draft, otherwise known as the skeleton. In this stage, you are simply trying to get everything down on paper. The ideas, the plot lines, the characters, their descriptions, their peccadilloes, their armadillos, the settings, the locales, the backstory, anything that pops into your head and sounds like it might be useful later. It's sort of like throwing everything at the wall and hoping something sticks.

After you've pieced together a skeleton that can walk and talk and sit and spin, it's time to add the muscle and the vital organs that make your book work. Adding life to your characters, details to your descriptions, humor if it's needed, sadness if it's not. Personal histories. Details. Physical descriptions. This layer improves upon the skeleton, often vastly. Now you can see the work as a whole piece. Not just this chapter or these few thousand words, but the whole enchilada, from tortilla to sour cream to salsa.

This is the time for you to act as an impartial reader, adding and taking away as you see fit. There can be no hard feelings, no "deal breakers." If something seems awkward to you, how do you think it will feel to your reader? Get rid of it. If a sentence is unruly, tweak it, rewrite it, fine tune it, or lose it (by that, I mean lose the sentence, not go postal). Don't worry about word count or whether or not you might have to go in and change a whole scene later. Just flesh things out to the best of your ability, then let it sit for a week or so until the next stage, called "Where the hell did I put my manuscript?"

Then you're ready to add the skin. The skeleton works, now it's got meat on its bones, and you're ready for that big, long, fat epidermal layer that covers everything up so no one can see your inner workings. You don't want readers to know where they're being taken, to see the innards of your story. You want them to flow along with you, not imagining who the suspect might be, not picking up on each and every clue, not second-guessing the bumbling detective. You want them surprised when they get there, and so you cover up the sinew and the guts and polish your story until it hums.

Finally, it's time for the last layer: the "dress-up" phase. Now's your chance to really shine. You've got the bulk of the story down, refined it, even fine-tuned it; here you get a chance to give it a real spit and polish. Get the phrasing just right. If a joke doesn't work, fix it. Try it out on friends. Your imagery, too. Test it all against your most scrutinizing and critical eye (probably your left one) and weed out anything that might detract from the seamless flow you've worked so hard to create.

▶ PROMPT: What object best represents you? Write about why.

The Power of Two

When you're not sure of where a scene should go, commit your-self to writing *two* versions. Or even three, if need be. Don't start by believing one will be better than the other; just think of them as two possible alternatives. This way, you can let go of the anxi-ety ("will this way work, or would it ruin my story?") and present yourself with two or three options that can be used or tossed. When should this happen? I tend to wait until the dress-up stage. After all, these two or three scene versions are like dress shirts you hold up to ties. Each one is good on its own merits, but only one is worthy of your final story. You won't be quite sure why you choose one over the other two, but you'll know it when you see it.

As a kid, I was crazy about those choose-your-own-ending books (at least until I discovered boys). I even wrote them in my youth. They weren't any good, of course (neither were a lot of the boys I discovered), but I was fascinated by the challenge of writing more than one fully fleshed-out ending. Now, I don't just apply this concept to my endings anymore. I apply it to any scene that doesn't have my complete confidence. And, interest-ingly, I recently got hired to write a choose-your-own-ending book about fairies.

So, if you're stuck on the scene where Joey has to decide whether to quit his job or stay, write it both ways. In the first, Joey quits and "finds himself" in a job he has secretly wanted since childhood. In the second, he sticks it out but challenges his boss about the thing that was making him want to leave. His boss is impressed by his gumption and gives him the promotion he deserved.

The beauty of this concept is that often one of your alterna-tive versions surprises you. In the example above, the second Joey is a much stronger character, one who stands his ground and solves his own problems without running away. It's an option that might not have occurred to me—ever—had I been rigid in my writing and not explored a second, or maybe a third, or even a fourth possibility.

This also applies to nonfiction work. Maybe you can't decide whether to start that article about abortion with the quote from the fifteen-year-old girl who just found out she was pregnant, or the statistics Planned Parenthood gave you about how girls of particular ethnicities have more unplanned pregnancies.

Either way could work, and they'd take your story into significantly different directions. But instead of fighting with yourself about which way you should go, agree to do the work and write it both ways. Does it seem like extra work? It is. But it's worthwhile, because at the end you'll have your answer.

And trust me, it will be the right answer because you won't be guessing. You'll have evidence right in front of you: both versions of the beginning of the piece. You can see for yourself—literally, see it—and be able to make a firm decision on which way reads better. Not *seems* better, but reads better. Now that's work worth doing, and work your editor is quite likely to appreciate.

This also works if you're at a stagnant point and have no darn idea where you're going next. Brainstorm about all of the possible ways your characters can get from point A to point B, and then write at least two of the versions.

Don't fence yourself in. Be open to new possibilities, new avenues to explore. Naturally, you won't want to write a scene full of bug-eyed aliens in your Western novel, but perhaps the "alien" turns into a stranger from out of town who does things much differently from our Western hero, thus shedding new light on both characters. See both versions as optional, and you'll be much more likely to take risks and, quite possibly, discover uncharted territories that add both depth and breadth to your work.

Take Baby Steps

If you're feeling overwhelmed by the thought of writing a whole novel, article, term paper, story, or whatever, break it down into small parts. You're not going to write the whole novel tonight. Tonight, you're just going to write one new scene, or one new page. To steal and mangle a popular twelve-step program catch-phrase, take it one word at a time.

It's making the commitment to put words down on paper, day after day, night after night, that turns pages into chapters, and chapters into books. But putting in the work consistently and on schedule doesn't just add words to your novel or true crime tome, it adds to your writing foundation. Yes, more metaphorical concrete.

It all adds to the wall you build around your talent, your profession, your proficiency, your writing. The wall that will eventually become harder and harder for the beast of writer's block to knock down.

You can also try writing your project as a letter. Just plop the words "Dear So-and-So" on top of your page, and begin writing as if you're composing a letter to a dear friend. It will make your writing more conversational, and should help it to flow easier. If your writing is intended to be more autobiographical, or if your character is telling the story in first person, try a new twist to this idea by plopping "Dear Diary" at the top of your page and watching the calculation and impasses disappear from your writing as it flows more freely from your fingers.

You Must Write the Hardest Thing to Write

Another way to achieve writer's block is not letting yourself write the very thing that is begging to come out.

When I was taking my first writing course in college, my first assignment was to write a memoir. We were supposed to write about a turning point in our lives. Immediately, one thought sprang to mind: I was raped as a little girl, and that was the thing that changed my life the most.

But almost just as quickly, another thought came in to squash it: "I can't write about *that!*" It was too personal. It would make me uncomfortable. It would make my professor uncomfortable. We'd both wind up feeling like we'd been sitting on vinyl bus seats bare legged on a really hot day. I would write about something safer instead.

So I got to work. The telling thing here is that I can't even remember now what I decided to write about. But I did choose something else, probably something relatively trivial, and I had a very hard time with it. It was my first lengthy case of writer's block. But I was (and am) your typical type-A personality—there was no way I was going to miss my deadline. I clutched my notebook, trying and trying to make words appear magically. I wrote a few stunted paragraphs here and there, but then I quickly scratched them out.

Way back in my mind something else was brewing: the memoir I was supposed to write.

I didn't want to write it. I was digging my heels in deep and flat out refusing to listen to that inner voice, sticking my fingers in my ears and shouting "la la la" whenever it tried to talk to me. I didn't want to take the risk and expose myself to this stranger—this professor I'd just met.

But then came the last day. One day before deadline, and all I had was a series of crossed-out paragraphs. And this memoir I was supposed to write was jumping up and down, saying, "Pick me! Pick me!"

All the energy it was taking to hold that idea down was sapping the small bit of energy I had to write the initial memoir.

There was this Jiminy Cricket in my head, looking over every banal sentence and saying, "This isn't what you're supposed to be writing. You have something much more important to write."

And so, just one night before the deadline, I threw away my scrap pages and started anew. I allowed the words that were pounding down the door to come out. They came out in a rush, tumbling over each other, vying to get down on the page.

Was I terrified? Thoroughly. When I was done, I wasn't sure if I could possibly turn it in. I felt like my skin had been removed and I was walking around all soft and exposed and kind of gross looking. But I somehow found the courage to hand over my pages. They were the last ones to go on the pile.

When the professor handed the papers back, mine was the only one he didn't return. Instead, he bent down and said quietly, "I want to see you after class."

"He hates it!" I was sure. "He's going to flunk me. He thinks I'm a melodramatic, deeply disturbed idiot who should drop out of this class right now and go straight into therapy. I'm worthless. And I'm bowlegged."

It's a little bit cruel to say "I want to see you after class" at the beginning of class (I think they learn that in teacher's college). I had to sit there, hot flashing and near tears, all the way through the end of class. And then, as everyone shuffled out, I thought I'd have an accident in my pants. I weakly stood and made my way to his desk, where he literally shook me by the lapels and told me I was going to be a writer.

That's the power of writing the thing that needs to be written. Do it.

"Do not, for money, turn away from all the stuff you have collected in a lifetime," says Ray Bradbury in *Zen in the Art of Writing*. "Do not, for the vanity of intellectual publications, turn away from what you are—the material within you which makes you individual, and therefore indispensable to others."

There is writing we have to do, like those magazine and newspaper assignments that we've contracted for and that might just end up paying the light bill. There is writing we think we need to do, like penning an ode to our dear old grandmother or writing another Christmas carol when the spirit hits us each December. There is writing we want to do, like when we see a new author pour out a string of back-to-back bestsellers in a new genre and think, "Why didn't I write those, apart from the fact that I know nothing about nuclear submarines?" And, finally, there is writing we *must* do, like the personal piece I just described.

It is the writing we must do that pours out of us almost effortlessly. That is the writing that tells itself, that flows together as if it had already been written deep down in our brains (next to the "Space for Rent" sign) and is just being set free. That is the writing that keeps us slogging through the midnight hour, desperate to catch every word on paper before it flits away from our fleeting consciousness. That is the writing you *must* be doing.

Ask yourself if you're writing the most urgent thing, the thing that you know, deep down, wants to come out. You must write that thing, whether you write it for publication or just for your own eyes, before you can take the next step as a writer.

If you don't, it will not only fester and mold with the ravages of time, but it could get in the way of the rest of your writing. Like that strong female lead who wouldn't get her big, fat nose out of my novel, the most urgent thing will always, always find a way to bubble to the surface in your everyday writing if you don't get it out of your system.

What's the thing that's burning a hole in the back of your brain, aside from you setting your hair alight with the curling iron again? What's the thing you're avoiding writing? The harder you're avoiding it, the more it needs to come out. As with most good writing, it has a mind of its own. It will come out, with or without you. It will pour out, when you least expect it. Better to control it, guide it, direct its power, passion and its evocative explosion out under your control, rather than vice versa. Dive right in head first. Just do it. Do it *now.* (Wait, no, come back. There's still one more section in this chapter.)

Your answer to writer's block may have been bubbling just beneath the surface all this time. Go see if it's ready to erupt yet.

▶ PROMPT: Your character is stuck—in an elevator, on a deserted island, in jail, on a plane, or wherever you like. He's stuck with the one person in the world he least wants to be stuck with. Who is it? Write a scene about what happens.

Parting with Your Words

If you know why you're blocked, and it's because you're bored with what you're writing and not a lack of dietary fiber, you have two choices: throw it away or change something drastically. Chances are good that if you're bored writing it, it's not working.

It's okay to throw away your work. It's frustrating, sure, but it's also liberating. If you've hit a dead end, it may be more pragmatic to toss it than to try to revive a flat-lined work. You have to decide whether you're up for a complete rewrite. If the answer is "no," you're probably too bored with the idea to do anyone any good. Don't hate your readers so much that you would force them to read something that couldn't even keep your own attention.

You're likely performing the literary equivalent of treading water. It was hard enough to put that first word down on paper, let alone the second, and the third, and then the first sentence, followed by that first paragraph, and then page after page full of your blood, sweat, and tears. (It's probably just as well to abandon it. Imagine trying to put that soggy mess in an envelope.) You figure you had the idea, you organized it in an outline however rough, and more than that, went on to flesh the idea out in a few pages, chapters, or sections.

Doesn't that mean it's worth finishing? Didn't your parents tell you never to be a quitter? Didn't your teachers tell you persistence pays off? After all, as the astute character Curly Howard from *The Three Stooges* advised, "If at first you don't succeed, keep sucking till you do suck seed!" Doesn't outwitting writer's block mean you just . . . keep . . . writing?

Well, not always. Sometimes it takes a bigger writer to stop writing something mediocre than to keep slogging through it just because he thinks he should, just for the sake of finishing it.

It's hard to part with the words we've worked so hard to put together. That's why some of us press on, even when we know we're getting nowhere. I once began a novel that had no real premise. I just decided one day that it was time I wrote a novel—it was either that or take out the garbage—so I started it. By about page five, I was already floundering. There was no skeleton holding this story together. And it didn't have the appeal of *Seinfeld*. It was just a novel about nothing—a whole series of clever descriptions and fragments of characters that never quite came together. But once I started it, I thought I should finish it, because I'm a good little girl who takes commitment seriously. So I kept writing, day after day, when I really should have quit and started something else instead.

No writing is ever done in vain; I'm sure my work improved through writing that never-finished novel. I learned about the importance of actually having a plot, at least. But I still wish I had stopped when I realized the story wasn't going anywhere, rather than forcing myself to continue just because I had put in so much time already.

In the song "Rock Bottom," Wynonna Judd sings, "A dead end street is just a place to turn around." So turn around. You have plenty of other things to write. Don't spend forever obsessing about a piece that doesn't merit more attention. Chalk it up to experience and move on.

A File for Misfits

This is where keeping that ongoing file (some would call it "circular") of false starts, half-finished stories, and rudimentary ideas comes in handy. When you have a place for these misfit pieces of flotsam and jetsam to call home, it doesn't quite seem like throwing them away. Even if you'll never ever look at them, when they're placed in something as important as a file, instead of something as lowly as a trash can, you can move on without guilt or hindrance.

Before I established a file for misfits, and despite the reams of pages, articles, stories, ideas, poems, diaries, and manuscripts I shredded, burned, and tossed into the circular file for years, I did somehow manage to trick myself into saving the odd gem here and there. The coming-of-age novel I wrote when I was, you guessed it, coming of age. The sweet romances I penned while I was falling in love. The edgy thrillers about murderous exes when I was finally dumped. The erotic free verse I wrote when I was . . . in between boyfriends. It's there, in hard copy, on a floppy disc, or stuck to my hard drive.

And I'm thankful. Why? Because I enjoy being embarrassed by something I wrote when I was fifteen? Because I enjoy torturing myself by reading aloud phrases such as "gag me with a spoon," "where's the beef?" and "you go, girl?" Because I can't get enough of peace signs and Duran Duran stickers all over my old notebooks and folders?

Nah. It's because when I'm blocked, when I'm stumped for new words, I can go back to the old. I take something out. Could be my famous "Ode to the Old Boyfriend in 6th Grade." Could be the lyrics to a song I wrote for John Denver. Could be that techno-thriller à la *Blade Runner* that I never finished because the necessary research into biosynthetic life forms got just a little too technical for my taste.

Doesn't matter. I take it out, I read it, I dry my eyes, and when my blush has finally receded several hours later, I take a new approach to this old material. I add to it, take away from it, rewrite it, tweak it, refresh it, update it.

I turn my old medical character à la Doogie Howser into a new medical character à la George Clooney. I turn my sexist Hardy Boys ripoff into a celebration of Nancy Drew. I reinvent that diary entry of my first U2 concert into an album review of their latest release. Who cares?

The point is: I'm writing. No, not that 900-word article that's due next Friday. No, not my latest screenplay. No, not even my grocery list. But it's still *creating*. It's fighting back that beady-eyed rodent, priming the pump, pounding the keyboard.

For that reason, I no longer throw anything away—no matter how embarrassing, revolting, or revealing it might seem to me two short weeks after writing it. I have a special storage area for such orphaned work. It may be work that got rejected one too many times by one too many publishers. It may be greeting card text that's too corny—or too edgy—for today's market trends. It may be a piece I did on spec that never got used ("The Complete Idiot's Guide to Watching Paint Dry"). It may be a manuscript that's not quite ready for the world—yet.

Either way, it's there when I need it. Waiting for me. A tool in my box filled with other items designed to cure writer's block. And now it's in yours as well.

Boredom comes in many shapes and sizes, and there's no doubt that lackluster writing is one very obvious result. But boredom doesn't have to be *all* bad. Maybe you wound up writing a bored character who becomes one of your favorites, at least when mixed in with a cast of more colorful cohorts in a project you're currently working on.

Maybe your boredom took on a manifestation that found you writing in a genre you're not accustomed to, but that you'd like to explore. Maybe that genre, and the couple hundred pages you wrote out of sheer boredom, deserves another look.

Maybe not. For the most part, writers who are bored produce writing that is boring. But when your block is over and you look at said writing in the light of a brand new day, it might just be salvageable after all.

And if not, all you lost in the effort was a little bit of time.

13

The Opposite Game

Letting Go When You've Outgrown Your Story

Some people believe that there's only one person in the world meant for them (unless they're guys, in which case they believe there's only one car, guitar, or fishing rod). Just one soul mate, and if you never find that person, you're doomed to a life of emptiness. That's a load of yams.

Just as I don't believe there's one single right person for you, I also don't believe there's just one way to tell your story. Love takes twists and turns; you may think you love someone's spontaneity, and later discover you can't stand how he or she can't plan ahead for anything. You may want to write a story about an abused woman, but later discover that you really think she's a wimpy idiot for not kicking her abuser in the groin.

You may find that you outgrow what initially attracted you to your story. You may grow tired of your characters' irksome habits, or get sick of visiting the same one-horse town every day. You've made no vow to love, honor, and cherish forever and ever, so you have nothing to feel guilty about if you abandon your story in favor of a younger model.

Look closely into the office of any writer, famous or unknown, young or old, rich or poor, and you are likely to see a hundred different drafts in a hundred different incarnations. What was once a short story written on spec—and never published—becomes a full-fledged novel. What started out as a novel became a novella, a novella became a screenplay, a screenplay became a documentary, and a documentary became a doorstop. Such is the writing life. There are hits, there are misses, and then there are hits that miss and misses that hit.

Along the way, it's natural to have a few false starts and to follow more than a couple of wrong turns. We're only human; it's just that writers tend to record their mistakes, often by the hundreds of pages!

▶ PROMPT: What is your character's phobia? Whether it's snakes, heights, public speaking, or the dark, what happens when she is confronted with this feared thing?

Playing the Opposite Game

Now, you may already have too much invested in your story to toss it altogether (it's too damned heavy!), or you may see its potential despite the fact that it just doesn't make you weak in the knees anymore (it's not heavy enough). In this case, it's time to play the opposite game.

Change the sex of your main character. Make that hunky mailman a dazzling mailwoman. Yes, I know this means a lot of work, and I know it changes your whole story. That's the point. It forces you to start again and take a completely fresh approach to your story.

For instance, what if, when you change your mailman to a mailwoman, his, er, *her* feelings don't change a whit for the romantic female lead? Talk about spicing things up a bit, not to mention frustrating all the men at the office ("The only two women we know, and they're both lesbians!"). Or, fine, you want her to be heterosexual. So now you have to change the sex of the romantic character, too. Yes, yes, it's more work. I *am* a taskmaster, after all. Consider it tough love.

Too radical? Change the setting. Move them out of the country and into the city, or vice versa. Pick a place you love to visit, or a place you've imagined you'd love to visit. Spend some mental time taking a vacation there. Talk to people who've been there. Take a virtual tour on the Internet. Call the state's tourism department and request brochures. You'll have a truckload of them on your doorstep before you know it.

A new setting may be just what you need to jump-start your story and deflate your writer's block. Maybe you're writing a thriller and wondering why it's not quite so thrilling. Well, changing the city scene to a mountainous terrain could just make your hero's daring escapes a lot more daring. After all, it's a little harder to sneak off a sheer rock cliff to escape the bad guys than it is to sneak out the back of a crowded diner.

Maybe your new setting is just what your story needs to set it apart from the rest of the field. Take the Amish theme out of the Harrison Ford hit movie *Witness* and you've got just another run-of-the-mill cop drama. But those bonnets and hardwood floors were more than just props; the setting became a character unto itself, living and breathing and taking up space as much as any of the actors. It colored what the actors did, made them say things differently, act differently, think differently. It was more than just a ploy, it was a brainstorm.

Perhaps playing the opposite game with your story's setting catapults it from so-so to so darn good you can't stop writing. These are just the types of experiments and alternatives that make the task, the profession, the *art* of writing a never-ending journey to truth and discovery. But it doesn't end there.

If you're stuck on a scene, move it. It doesn't have to move out of state, just change rooms. Move your characters from the living room into the bedroom, from the kitchen into the backyard, from the bar to the roller rink (though they really shouldn't skate if they've been drinking). Use contrast to your advantage; let your characters have that terrible fight at a carnival or bridal shower instead of at the restaurant. Let them have their gloriously happy reunion in a hospital. Let the setting be so contradictory that it only highlights the mood—that the mood exists against all odds. Everything in your story should happen "against all odds."

Change from first person to third person or vice versa. Change from past tense to present tense. Add bookends to your story: an old man in a nursing home reciting his tale to a young boy. The beginning is the young boy coming to visit Grandpa, the middle is the story itself, and the end is the young boy walking away transcended through his grandfather's amazing tale. Tell your story in letters, in e-mails, in phone calls, in Instant Messages, on cocktail napkins left in the ladies' room. Shake things up.

When you think your character has gone through all he or she can go through, raise the stakes. Then do it again and again. Think about what your character would fear most in the world (spiders, heights, the McDonald's McRib sandwich), and then make it happen.

What Raising the Stakes Means

Most writers have heard the advice that you should make life as difficult as possible for your character, like the IRS does. However, a frequent problem is that new writers often interpret this to mean, "Write a whole series of bad things that happen to my character." So we get stories about mothers who get caught in traffic, then lose their kid in the park, then get their wallet stolen, then have their brother die . . . This is not raising the stakes. This is just a series of unconnected bad things that don't necessarily teach us anything new about the character.

Raising the stakes means that you show the character has a lot to lose, then you take him to the verge of losing it all. It may be a literal life-or-death situation, or it may mean losing the thing he holds dearest (his children, his morality, the house he built himself, his wife, his health). Maybe he's a marathon runner who gets into an accident that may leave him paralyzed. For this to work, you have to show us why running is so important to him—it can't be just his job or hobby; it has to hold deep personal meaning for him that readers can understand.

Now raise the stakes even higher. Not only is he hearing the news that he may never run again, but while in the hospital, he gets a letter from the daughter who ran away from home when she was sixteen and disappeared from his life. It turns out she's getting married and wants him to walk her down the aisle. She doesn't know about his accident, and he can't bear the thought of being in a wheelchair when they're finally reunited. He has to *walk* her down the aisle. Now he has an even deeper reason to rehabilitate himself.

A character's goals don't always have to be met neatly. Your characters should wind up getting even more than they intended—and not necessarily in the manner they wanted it. (As Richard J. Needham said: "God punishes us mildly by ignoring our prayers and severely by answering them.") Your hero, a police officer, may think his main goal is to bust a high-profile drug dealer. But in doing so, he may find out his own son is on drugs. Whether or not your hero nails the "bad guy" isn't so important anymore—what becomes more important is straightening out his son and forming an honest father-son relationship.

Don't plan to have a moral of the story. If there is one, it should evolve naturally from the story line, not the other way around.

▶ PROMPT: Write a scene that ends with two people making up after a long misunderstanding that kept them apart.

Quick Fixes When You're Stalled

Take a Break

Another quick way to outwit writer's block is to take a break from the project you're working on (no, staring out the window is *not* a project) and do something radically different, even for fifteen minutes. (Within reason, of course. Yes, becoming a go-go dancer *is* radically different, but totally impractical in this case. You wouldn't even have time to do your makeup!) If you're working on an article, stop and make up a limerick. If you're working on a novel, stop and write a greeting card, letter, poem, or song lyrics. Take just fifteen minutes away and commit to taking your mind completely off the original project. You never know what you'll come up with.

Don't Be Yourself

Your mom told you to "just be yourself." Now toss that advice and be someone else. After all, she also told you Santa Claus was real and needles didn't hurt. If you're feeling really stuck, pretend you're a completely different person—a writer you admire, or just someone with a lot more self-confidence, and when you sit down to write, embody this new personality. If you're a woman, be a man. If you're a man, be a woman. Be someone with more or less education—though you may not want to pretend to be illiterate. Be someone with a different cultural background. Be someone older or younger. Commit to your new "self" the way an actor commits to a role.

You may also want to try "method writing": become one of your characters.

Spend a day, or even a week, living in your character's shoes. I once spent days living as my character Seianna Russo, an inexperienced photographer who has a habit of letting people step all over her. I let everyone behind me at the "ten-items-or-less" checkout go in front of me with their twenty boxes of cereal ("It's all the same thing, so it only counts as one item"). When in traffic, I slowed to let people cut me off. I held the door for everyone and didn't get annoyed when people failed to say "thank you." The pay phone ate my quarter and I didn't call the operator to complain. I just went back later and took to it with a sledgehammer.

I wanted to become this character to get a better understanding of her everyday life. I needed to know how it felt to be meek and giving to a fault. When I returned to the keyboard, I had a whole host of new experiences to write about. Now I knew the way people look at you when you slouch and have trouble making eye contact. I knew what my character would say when someone pronounced her name wrong—nothing. She might even apologize for having a hard-to-pronounce name.

If you want to get to know your characters better, become them. Dress like them, talk like them, engage in activities they'd enjoy. And don't quit when those nice young men in their clean white coats come to take you away. Just find out what your character would do in that situation.

Opposite Situations

Another way to play with opposites is to completely alter your writing environment. If you're used to working with music in the background, try working in silence. Or change types of music from classical to show tunes, or rock to opera. If you normally work in sweatpants, dress in formal attire when you set out to write this time. Drink tea instead of your usual soda (or whatever you're telling everyone it is).

Change rooms, change times, change lighting. Write in the dark, so you can't see what you're writing. (I once did a series of charcoal drawings with the lights out—I called them my "Art in the Dark" series—and was surprisingly pleased with the results.)

Whatever you do, shake things up. Your current method isn't working, so you have to change something. Accept that, and experiment to find what works. You might just find out that even though you normally work better in silence, this time, you need the background sounds of a CD to keep you going.

Add a Prop

Find out if you can develop a special piece of attire or "prop" to signify that it's writing time. I have a special floppy hat I like to wear when I'm writing. It's a little like Dumbo's feather: sure, I could fly without it (as long as I had the right medication), but it's a fun prop to have. It's my writer hat. I'm wearing it right now.

I know a writer who writes in the nude. I haven't been quite so bold yet, but if you are, why not try it? Especially if you're writing love scenes.

You might try hanging a "writer-at-work" sign over your desk, wearing a special pin, or having a stuffed animal or slippers that come out only when it's time to write. Your brain will form a connection between that object and writing time.

Play Cards

Here's another exercise I want you to try when you're blocked.

I want you to buy a pack of at least 100 index cards. Break them up into six piles: two with ten cards, the rest with twenty cards. Leave one pile of ten cards to the side—forget about them for now.

On the other pile of ten cards, I want you to write character names (on the lined side, if you bought lined index cards). Hopefully, these are characters you've already developed, at least somewhat. If you haven't, spend a few minutes writing short descriptions of each of these ten characters. You should at least know a bit about their personalities, background, employment, marital status, and passions.

On the next pile (twenty cards), you're going to write one-line descriptions of actions. These shouldn't be boring, everyday acts (like sleeping, walking, or getting dressed). They should be the kind of actions you'd write about in your journal—things you'd want to remember. Examples: singing in public, almost drowning while skinny-dipping, consulting a psychic, riding a motorcycle, dying your hair blue, or getting stuck in an elevator.

On the next pile, write settings. Choose a variety of both big and small places; wide locations (like New Jersey) and specific places (a catering hall). Examples: neighbor's backyard, an airport, bathroom, a park, Australia, or a cemetery.

The next pile is for objects and supporting characters. Write the names of twenty inanimate objects, props, and/or people/pets that could factor into a story. Examples: a whip, a dog, old bully from grade school, sports car, or nail polish.

The next pile is for emotions. Again, choose a wide range: anger, exhilaration, shock, sadness, embarrassment, or satisfaction, which all work.

Now pick up that last pile of ten that I told you to put aside. These are your wild cards (so watch out that they don't bite you). If you were on a roll with any particular category and ran out of cards before you ran out of ideas, this is your chance to write more. Use those cards in any way you wish; add them to the other piles when you're done.

Now comes the fun part. Shuffle each pile of cards and pick one from each pile (no peeking). Your job is to write a story incorporating all five items. The star of your story is the character you chose. He or she will do the action in the place you selected, and the object or supporting character will feature prominently in the story. The emotion can be the general mood of the story, or the character's emotion about the event.

Using my examples above, I might have selected a story about a young lady named Sheila who sings in public in a neighbor's backyard with a whip and feels angry about it. Why would she be singing with a whip in a neighbor's backyard? Well, maybe she just picked up a part-time job doing singing telegrams. She's there to give a "naughty" happy birthday to her neighbor. But she's angry about it, because she recently broke up with the neighbor's son and she tried to call in sick, but her boss threatened to fire her if she didn't show up.

Not all of the cards will fit so neatly together, however. I might just as easily have selected a story about my character Ryan who almost drowns while skinny-dipping at an airport with a dog and feels exhilaration. Doesn't quite work, except maybe as a farce, right? This is where you get to take creative license. Okay, so Ryan can't logically skinny-dip at an airport (without getting into a *lot* of trouble). But how can the airport remain a part of this story? Maybe he's skinny-dipping with a girl he has to take to the airport in a half hour. The dog jumps in after them because he thinks they're drowning. He expects to feel miserable when he takes her to the airport, because she's leaving for the whole summer. But instead, he feels exhilarated because while they were skinny-dipping, she told him she loved him for the first time, even though the water was extremely cold.

It's a little like Mad Libs, but you're creating the whole story. So get your creative juices in shape, and see where your cards take you!

Starting in the second grade, I loved writing, whether it was keeping a diary or writing long newsy letters to Grandma. But as I got older, teachers, family members, and an ex-spouse all dismissed my writing as a waste of time. So later, when it came time to writing something for publication, my brain froze. How could I bare my soul and put it out there for people to make fun of like my family and friends had? I spent a couple of years in frozen inertia with a major case of writer's block until . . . I developed multiple personalities. I decided I needed to become somebody else: somebody who could write.

I have B. Lee Workman, who's young and sensitive and writes poetry. She's had several nature poems published. Then I have Fiona Woods, who writes fiction. She's a little older than Lee and more imaginative. She's had two short stories published. Last I have Barbara L. Workman, who writes nonfiction. She writes about her family and life experiences, and has been published in national magazines like Woman's World.

All three writers have won awards for their writing; however, nobody knows all three are really me. If you're looking for fame, this isn't the way to go. But if you're looking for the way out of writer's block, give it a try. It just might work for you, too!

—Barbara L. Workman, writer

14

Mind Your Own Business

Writing Is a Job

The best cure for writer's block is the timeless advice: "Apply seat of pants to chair." In the end, writing is a job just like any other—you have to show up, and you have to produce.

As personal an act as writing is, you must learn to see your work as a separate entity after it is done. While you're writing it, sure, it's an extension of you. But once you're through with it, you can't let your self-image be wrapped up in what others think of it.

When someone rejects a piece of your writing, they're rejecting *it*, not you. This is an important distinction. You are not your writing. Each piece is only one small part of who you were at the time you wrote it. If one of your projects isn't working, it doesn't mean you have failed. It only means that you haven't yet solved a problem with a particular piece of writing.

Not every editor will choose to use your talents, and not every reader will be bowled over by your words. Reading taste is highly subjective, and if you're setting out to please everyone, you're likely to come out with a very bland writing style. Don't aim to appease everybody; aim to thrill the people who will "get" your work. To heck with the rest of the world.

Now comes the harshest thing I'm going to say in this book: no one said you had to be a writer. You chose it. Now you have to choose to do the things that go along with being a writer; namely, you have to write.

Do whatever it takes to make this happen. If you're going to be a full-time writer, you don't have the luxury of having writer's block for any extended period of time. Your brain may be full of rocks and petroleum jelly, but you are still required to coax words onto the page.

"Over the years, I've found one rule," says Norman Mailer in *The Spooky Art.* "It's a simple rule. If you tell yourself that you are going to be at your desk tomorrow, you are by that declaration asking your unconscious to prepare the material. You are, in effect, contracting to pick up such valuables at a given time. Count on me, you are saying to a few forces below: I will be there to write. The point is that you have to maintain trustworthy relations. If you wake up in the morning with a hangover and cannot get to literary work, your unconscious, after a few such failures to appear, will withdraw."

▶ PROMPT: Have you ever had an out-of-body experience? Seen a ghost? Had a psychic vision? Believed you were saved by a guardian angel? Write about a striking other-worldly experience and how it changed you. If not, write about what it might be like.

Change Your Environment

So, what to do when you're on deadline and so blocked you can't even write your name?

In short: go away. Change your environment completely. Do something drastic. Rent a hotel room or cottage for the weekend. If you have a laptop, great. If not, paper and pens still work (hint: use the pointy end).

Sometimes, changing your environment can break the stagnation. I know writers who've found that getting away for a weekend completely recharges them. No ringing phone, no kids running around, no laundry to be done. Your brain can be completely freed up to concentrate only on the job at hand, rather than your everyday responsibilities.

If there's no way you can leave for a weekend, at least get out for the day. Go to the park with your favorite notebook. Bring bread for the ducks if you so desire, but don't let yourself get too sidetracked. You're here on a mission.

Get More Quotes

Often, what's broken my block when working on a nonfiction article is a gem of a quote. Sometimes all it takes is a few wise words from an expert to get me thinking of new angles and new areas to discuss. You can never do too many interviews. I once conducted more than 100 interviews for a 900-word article. It's one of the best I've ever written.

When planning out your interviews, look outside of the obvious choices. For an article about violence in children's movies, you might think to interview child psychologists, filmmakers, and people who've conducted studies relevant to this topic, such as a representative from Harvard School of Public Health. But what about parents, screenwriters, the Motion Picture Association of America, a juvenile detention center officer, children, and teachers?

You never know which one is going to come up with that fabulous quote that will tie your whole story together. The teacher may comment on how the kids in her class misbehaved more after they all saw *Home Alone*. The child may casually talk about the way the Power Rangers beat people up. The juvenile detention center officer may make the astute observation that children who already show a propensity toward violence tend to gravitate toward violent movies—not that they become violent only after seeing the movies.

Always err on the side of gathering too much information rather than too little. You don't have to use all of it—you may choose to quote only one or two people in the final article—but you'll be in a position to cherry-pick. Let the experts do some of the work for you.

When you're working, try to take a ten-minute break every hour. Get up and stretch, have a snack, listen to some music, and give your brain a break. It's difficult to concentrate on one thing for more than an hour at a time, and you may find the block digging its heels in deeper if you force the wheels in your mind to keep spinning long after your optimum concentration period is over.

Recognizing When Your Work Is Done

There comes a time in every writer's life when it's time to let go of your babies and let them move out on their own.

"I have to admit that I am dreadfully anal about rewriting and I have a hard time letting go of the manuscript at the end, even though at that point I am often sick of it," says acclaimed children's author Rachna Gilmore. "I know that I can always make it that one bit better, even if it is to tweak a sentence, or to change one word to another just a bit more apt."

Indeed, it seems there's always one more word you could change, one more mother-in-law joke you could add, one more sentence you could cut. But there has to be a time when you are at peace with your work and recognize that it's ready. It's done.

It has to be done sometime—and only you can make the call as to when. But realize that no bell will sound, no clock will be punched, and no fat lady will sing. It's just a decision you have to reach quietly, when you've edited and proofread and believe there's no more to be done.

You may feel separation anxiety when it's time for the manuscript to leave the safety of your computer. After all, this has been your baby (born of immaculate conception). Your personal project, safe from the cruel outside world, save for that damn virus that nearly erased it. And now you have to hand it over to someone who may not see it through a mother's eyes. Someone who may not think its facial birthmark is endearing. You may feel protective of your words, unsure of your readiness to hear that it's anything less than perfect. Besides, the moment you let it go, you'll have to start all over with the blank page again. And you may be reluctant to put yourself through the process again; you may be stalling to avoid starting a new project. But somehow, you summon the courage. Don't worry: telling your real kids to leave home will be a lot easier, especially when they start wanting to borrow the car.

Expect that the most regret you will ever feel as a writer is at the moment you send your manuscript to an editor. Instantly, you will find one more typo. One more word that just doesn't "sound" right. It's like a practical joke played on all writers; that last typo will remain invisible until the instant the manuscript has been sent out. You will cringe. You will think this editor will gasp in horror and throw your manuscript into the nearest furnace, lighting it especially for this occasion if necessary. You will believe your career is over.

"Should I send a follow-up e-mail?" you'll wonder. "Maybe I could chase down the mailman and steal back my package? I don't *think* he's armed." But no. You must resist. You must trust that the editor will find and eradicate that last typo, and that her entire opinion of your work will not rest on that one word. You have to have a little more faith both in your writing and in those reading it.

To more fully enjoy a sense of closure, there's a skill you should practice: don't read your work after you send it out. I know, it's damn-near irresistible, especially when the editor hasn't responded and you're dying to figure out why—so you reread your manuscript, looking for all the possible reasons why the editor is probably laughing her head off as she passes it to her colleagues and exclaims, "This kind of writing would make a blind man claw his eyes out! Anyone know how to light this furnace?"

That's when you find that blasted typo. And then you start to think that maybe the rest of your manuscript isn't all that good either. In fact, the first paragraph is kind of overdone, and there are at least three clichés, and the ending is too predictable. If only you had your own furnace! And you hide under the covers, wishing you'd gone to Katherine Gibbs and learned a trade, wondering if you can still catch the plague and die quietly before you're blacklisted in the writing industry.

But then a miracle happens somewhere along the line: your work gets accepted. O glorious day! You celebrate. You drink too much. You tell yourself in slurred speech that you knew, deep down, that your writing was really genius and that that typo didn't matter. You pretend you had faith in yourself all along.

And this euphoria lasts all the way until you get your page proofs. Then your bipolar disorder kicks in. Suddenly, you plunge into the depths of despair again.

It seems that evil, illiterate gnomes have come in and changed all of your words when you weren't looking. Certainly, these couldn't have been the words you wasted a whole bottle of wine on. These words are boring, uninspired, old. You can write much better now. You want to throw out the whole thing, apologize to the editor, and start from scratch. But you can't, because these are page proofs, and the only thing you're supposed to do now is take one last look to make sure there are no typos or factual errors.

You think about breaking into the editor's office and stealing her files, replacing them with brand new ones. But you're not all that secure in your skills as a burglar. Writers are rarely good at burgling. You can't even break into your own car when you lock your keys in there. (Does that coathanger trick ever actually work for anyone?)

So you have no other choice: you have to let go. You have to let those words, imperfect as they may be, find their way into the world. You must trust the part of yourself that knew you were done, and devote yourself, instead, to the next project and the next.

Let your baby be grown. Even if you're sure he can't cook for himself, will never pay the electric bill on time, and will only call when he needs money. You'd be amazed at how much those babies can actually do, even when you think they're not ready to leave the roost.

Letting go is never easy. It's so final. That self-doubt that haunts you, however, is the flip side of the thing that makes you a better writer: perfectionism. You want your words to be just right, which is why you strive for excellence. That's why you worry after your work has been accepted for publication—you can never be absolutely sure that you've risen to the challenge and produced excellent work.

▶ PROMPT: Invent a new word, then write a poem about it.

Compare You to You

One of the most difficult things about being a writer is that there is no accurate measuring stick to tell you how good you are. There are no right and wrong words, no tests to pass. Plumbers know when they've done a good job immediately, because they've just made two hundred bucks plus parts changing a washer so the sink no longer leaks. But writers depend on feedback from editors, reviewers, and readers to know if they've succeeded, and you'll never get a 100 percent feedback rate (that is, most of your readers won't write to tell you what they thought of your work). Therefore, it's up to you to gauge how good a job you're doing.

Rather than comparing yourself to other writers, compare yourself today to you last year, five years ago, ten years ago. Do you write more effectively now? Have you honed your skills? That's something to applaud. Give yourself permission to be proud. It's not easy for most of us to accept compliments, especially from ourselves, but in a field like writing, it's imperative that you learn to give yourself praise when you write well, or when you improve your discipline, finish a project, or have a productive writing session. ("That was really good, Jenna." "You think so, Jenna?" "Absolutely.")

Being published is positive reinforcement, but in the long term, it can't be the *only* positive reinforcement. You must be satisfied with your life, and the validation that comes with being published won't be enough to sustain you for all your years to come. Foremost, you must feel rewarded by the act of writing.

There are countless talented writers who will never be published. Therefore, publication itself can't be the measuring stick by which you count your achievements. A work may not be published in an author's lifetime because of publishing trends, timing, similar works already on the market, and a thousand other factors that have nothing to do with the quality of the writing. Does that mean the writer has wasted his or her life? Not if the act of writing was satisfying to that writer.

Your Writing Oasis

15

Claiming Your Writing Space

Your writing space should be uniquely you. Messy or organized, isolated or bustling with energy, it should serve to assist your creativity.

Most writers prefer to have their own personal nook in the house that's dedicated to their work. Of course, if you have a home office, you're ahead of the game. But if not, consider partitioning off a section of a room for yourself. Hang a curtain or tapestry, and make actual boundaries that you can enter and exit. You can even build yourself a fort of couch cushions.

I find it amusing that most writers I know are messy by nature—me included—but most also agree that cleaning up helps writing flow better. If your surroundings are crowded and scattered, your brain will be crowded and scattered.

Even if cleaning's not your thing, give it a shot. Buy a filing cabinet and get all of those contracts and random papers filed away in an orderly fashion.

Using Feng Shui

Feng shui means "wind and water." It's not a newfangled religion; it's an ancient Chinese practice that aims to best use space and environment for optimal health, wealth, happiness, relationships, creativity, and knowledge. Practitioners call it an "art of placement," which basically means they move stuff around in the hopes of changing your life. That's what earthquakes are—Mother Nature doing a bit of feng shui. Luckily, you don't have to know a whole lot about it to start using its teachings for your benefit. There are a number of quick and dirty cures you can enact right now to set up your work space for better *chi*.

"The beneficial energies are known as 'chi,' which are the invisible vibes that give life to all beings," says Suan, subeditor of *Feng Shui Times* (www.fengshuitimes.com). "Positive 'chi' is good feng shui, negative 'chi' is bad feng shui. Good feng shui enhances your life to the maximum as allowed by destiny and luck. You know your house or office has good feng shui when everything is smooth and goes your way; everyone is healthy and happy. You know you need to do something about your home/office's feng shui when accidents keep happening, business transactions fail, you get sick, et cetera."

According to the principles of feng shui, you should never have your back facing a door directly—even if you don't realize it, this setup can leave you feeling vulnerable. If you want power and security, you'll want to have the widest viewpoint possible. Rather than letting someone enter your room without you knowing, you should set up your desk and chair in a manner so you can see the door, at least from your peripheral vision. If this is impossible, put a small mirror in your range of vision, and angle it so you can see the doorway. (Just make sure the mirror isn't showing a reflection of clutter.) You may also want to put a bell on the door, so you hear when someone is about to come in.

Whenever possible, your desk should have a solid wall behind it (to represent your career's "solid backing"), and it should not be in a corner if you want to avoid stagnated *chi* (you may have been sitting in a corner all through school, but you're allowed to come out now). Be sure you're not sitting under a beam, or even directly under a light, if possible. "Be aware of your surroundings; make sure that there are no sharp corners pointing at you," says Suan. "This may affect your well-being and you may feel uneasy or have this nagging feeling that something is doing you harm. And you won't be able to write properly."

To add positive energy to your work space, try hanging a symmetrical, clear crystal. You can hang it by your window, or put it on a stand on your bookshelf. Likewise, healthy plants also add positive energy. Even the legal ones.

If you're having trouble differentiating between your work space and your living space, try placing wind chimes in the doorway of your work space. Hearing the wind chimes should be a signal to you that you are leaving one environment and coming into a new one, with fresh energy. Feeling them smacking you in the face should signal you that you've hung them too low. Also, make sure you don't have to step over or around anything to get to your work space; this is considered an obstruction of *chi*.

Heavy—or symbolically heavy—objects can help you feel "grounded." If you're feeling flighty or unfocused and want to try a feng shui cure, you can either adopt an elephant, or, if you're not quite so fond of cleaning up droppings the size of Buicks, you can buy an elephant statue.

If possible, change from fluorescent lighting to full-spectrum lighting. You want to mimic natural lighting as much as possible without blasting a hole in your roof. The glare of your computer screen probably leaves you feeling tired and headachy after a while, so it's even more important to have good lighting when you're working at the computer for long stretches of time.

Color also plays an important role in feng shui. Black is said to reduce energy; whereas red may overactivate your energy.

Flowing water is said to be good for attracting money. (Did I just see some ears perk up?) You can achieve this by having a small fountain or fish tank in your work space.

▶ PROMPT: Rewrite a nursery rhyme. You can write a parody, a modernized version, or a just-loosely-based-on story in a different format (e.g., write it as a play, a personal essay by one of the characters, etc.).

Your Kua Number

Here's what Suan had to say about curing writer's block:

You should find out your best directions and if possible, use them to the fullest. This is called 8 Mansions (Pa Chai), a feng shui method that is easy and efficient. Using 8 Mansions, here is how to calculate your Kua number:

For males: take the last two digits of the year of your birth and add them. If it's not a single digit, add those two digits together. Then subtract the digit from 10.

For example, for a male born in the year 1967:

$6 + 7 = 13$
$1 + 3 = 4$
$10 - 4 = 6$

So for a male born in 1967, his Kua number is 6.

For females: do the same with the last two digits of the year of your birth and then add 5.

For example, for a female born in the year 1967:

$6 + 7 = 13$
$1 + 3 = 4$
$4 + 5 = 9$

So for a female born in 1967, her Kua number is 9.

However, males who obtain the number 5 should refer to Kua 2 and females who obtain the number 5 should refer to Kua 8 [there is no Kua 5].

The grouping and best direction (Sheng Qi) for each Kua:

East Group:	West Group:
Kua 1: Southeast	Kua 2: Northeast
Kua 3: South	Kua 6: West
Kua 4: North	Kua 7: Northwest
Kua 9: East	Kua 8: Southwest

Armed with your Kua number, use a compass to determine the directions of your work space. Try to sit and work facing your best direction (Sheng Qi). It is also beneficial if you could work in a room that is located in your best direction. For example, a Kua 8 should work facing southwest in a room in the southwest sector of the house.

If possible, try to sleep with your head pointing to your good direction as well.

—Suan

More on the Feng Shui Way

Did that confuse you? Well, lucky for us, there's an online calculator that'll speed up the whole process. Visit www.dragon-gate.com/members/kuaCalculator/index.asp for a "Kua calculator" that will automatically figure out your Kua number for you and make feng shui suggestions based on it. For example, my Kua number is 8, and the site told me to put an aquarium with six goldfish and one black fish in the Southwest of my home. Um . . . okay.

You can also check out these Web sites:

Feng Shui Ultimate Resource: www.qi-whiz.com

World of Feng Shui: www.wofs.com

Feng Shui Help: www.fengshuihelp.com

Clearing Clutter

And here's a point for even those who think this whole "feng shui thing" is just too weird: clearing the clutter out of your life (and especially out of your work space) is just as important. "Too much clutter around you does indeed clutter your mind," says Suan. "There are no mystical applications to it; it is just from a psychological viewpoint that you get frustrated when there are too many things around and you just can't get down to it."

Use Your Environment to Enhance Your Creativity

Take a look around you and see if you can change anything to better enhance your creativity. Even your computer desktop wallpaper and screen saver can be used as tools to improve your concentration and focus. If you're looking at a background of boring boxes, try switching your wallpaper to something scenic and inspiring, like a waterfall. You can also change your screen saver to "word art" and have it scroll a message to you, such as "You are the world's greatest writer" or a favorite quotation about writing.

I even bought a "writer mug." You can find them on-line—try my store at www.cafepress.com/writegear, or the RexTechs store for technical writers at www.cafepress.com/techwriters.

Anything you can do to visually remind yourself that you're a writer is a good thing.

Look Right Before Your Eyes

When you're stuck for a new idea, take a tip from humorist John Cantu. In his article, "Writer's Block? Look Around You and Create," published at Cantu Humor (www.humormall.com), he writes, "One of the principles I have been teaching for years is when you have writer's block, look around you for inspiration" "I'd say, 'Simply look at the overhead light bulb or easy chair across the room, or the papers on your desk, or the carpet on the floor, or the wastebasket. Look and ask yourself questions and write down the answers that pop into your head.'"

And he means that quite literally. He suggests that you ask yourself these questions: "Who might use this light bulb?" "Who might buy this light bulb?" "Who might sell this light bulb?" "Who might replace this light bulb?" "What else or who else is connected with this light bulb?"

"Looking at the light bulb may remind you about a humorous electrical repair experience you had forgotten or may kick off something about the frustration of paying your utilities bill," he says.

You can try this exercise with any object you see. Imagine the factory where your telephone came from. Think about the workers who spend eight hours a day, five days a week, just assembling phones. Imagine the operator and what her day might be like. Think of all the wacky, scary, and prank phone calls the operator gets every day. Imagine why someone would be waiting for the phone to ring, or dreading its ring. What would life be like if the telephone had never been invented? What is a telemarketer's life like?

You can also try this with your body. When I pack my luggage for a trip, I always do a "body check," starting with the top of my head and working down to my feet. I think about what I need for my hair (shampoo), then my face (soap), my nose (allergy medicine), my mouth (toothbrush), and so on. You can do the same thing with your writing brainstorming.

Start at the top: your hair. You could write an article about the different products meant to stop hair loss, or a short story about a woman who has decided to shave off all her hair. Next comes your brain. You could write an essay about taking care of a parent with Alzheimer's disease, an article about raising a gifted child, or a screenplay about someone who has figured out how to use the 90 percent of the human brain that the rest of us don't use.

Go all the way down to your toes (an article about getting rid of nail fungus, an erotic story about a person with a foot fetish, or a poem about how you adore your partner's imperfect piggies).

This exercise is a great excuse to keep your writing oasis stocked with interesting things. Go ahead and buy that gaudy elephant statuette—it'll inspire you to write about the circus, or animal rights—or yo-yo dieting. ("Honey, I *needed* that elephant statue! I already wrote about everything else in the room!")

You can also look out your window and tell the story of the jogger, the door-to-door salesman, or the squirrel.

At this rate, you'll never have "nothing to write about" again. Time to think up another excuse for sitting in front of the television.

Branching Out

16

Choosing a Different Form

Writers put restrictions on themselves with labels such as "poets," "screenwriters," "romance authors," and so on. Maybe your so-called novel is a screenplay dying to get out. Maybe your book is really an article, once you reduce the font to normal size. Never allow a label to restrict you.

One of the reasons you could be blocked is because you've chosen the wrong form. After all, who said you should write for *National Geographic*? Who said you could only write biographies of dead white men? Who told you to write screenplays, TV commercials, true crime books, or greeting cards?

▶ PROMPT: Write about a family tradition that is uniquely yours.

Articles and Nonfiction Books

If you're writing an article, and you can't figure out how you'll fit in everything you need to say, maybe you should be writing a nonfiction book. Articles are meant to be narrow in scope; books are appropriate for bigger topics. If you're writing an article, ask yourself if you have an angle. You can't possibly write about "how to attract a man" in one article, but you can write about "how to use body language to attract a man." (Answer: sign the words "I like watching football.") With articles, the key is to think smaller. Pick one small aspect of a topic and go into it in detail, rather than trying to give an overview of a larger topic.

Conversely, if you're writing a book and don't feel like you have enough to fill the pages, consider writing it as an article or a series of articles instead. This happened to me not long ago. I thought I had a great idea for a nonfiction book and decided to pitch it to a publisher who I knew specialized in just this type of story. I spent a week or two composing a first-rate book proposal, researching my competition, and writing a sample chapter so the publisher could envision how the book might read.

Not long after I sent it, I got a very polite personal rejection letter (the worst kind, because it's hard to hate the person who wrote it) thanking me for my book proposal. The editor went on to say that she didn't feel the book was quite strong enough to carry 200 to 250 pages on its own merit, but that she felt it would make a great article. Accordingly, she gave me the name of the senior editor at a magazine that was owned by the same publisher. Currently, I'm completing the article for publication early next year.

And so it goes. I was darned sure that the subject matter was plenty stimulating enough for a book when I sent it off to that publisher. But upon further reflection—and one thoughtful rejection—I had to agree with that considerate editor. The "meat" for a book—let alone a mass audience—just wasn't there. After the initial excitement about penning an entire book wore off, the thought of writing an article on the same subject matter just made sense. That it took an outsider to point this out to me just goes to show you that no matter how far along you are in your writing career, there is always someone available to show you that you're just not quite as far along as you'd like to think.

To find markets for your articles, buy yourself a copy of this year's *Writer's Market* (an annual guide published by Writer's Digest Books—the on-line version at www.writersmarket.com is well worth the money, too), and visit these Web sites: Absolute Markets (www.absolutemarkets.com), Freelancing 4 Money (www.freelancing4money.com), Writers Weekly (www.writersweekly.com), and Funds for Writers (www.fundsforwriters.com).

Screenplays and Plays

If your idea is primarily visual, it's probably a screenplay. Screenplays are action driven. There must be a good reason why your story must be told on a big screen; my rule of thumb is that if it could be told on a page instead (as a novel, novella, or short story), then it probably should be. The written screenplay is a mere blueprint. Your story must be easily pictured as a series of exciting shots if you expect someone to invest millions of dollars into making it. Either that, or you have to have a long-lost uncle named Francis Coppola.

Christina Hamlett, author of *ScreenTEENwriters*, suggests that you don't rent headsets the next time you're on a plane with an in-flight movie to test Alfred Hitchcock's idea that the best films are ones you can watch without sound. "We don't have to watch one for very long to figure out who's being chased, who's doing the chasing, and who's falling in love in between," she says.

A misconception about screenplays is that they're dialogue driven. They're not. That's what plays are for. If your story only takes place in a few locations and doesn't require special effects or big car chases, it may be a play. Plays are more similar to television sitcoms or dramas than they are to screenplays. They both hinge on compelling dialogue between characters (or in some cases, monologue). "In a novel, we get to know the characters pretty intimately because we can literally read their thoughts and emotions at every juncture," says Hamlett. "In a play, we learn about them gradually through the course of their conversations; we only know what they're thinking, though, if they actually express it out loud to someone else or in a monologue."

The action in a play is much smaller in scope than the action in a screenplay. Just because of logistics, you can't have your characters on a Ferris wheel, a jet ski, or in a fire (unless there's an electrical problem backstage), and you can't have overwhelmingly large crowd scenes or lots of "bit players" (actors with no more than a line or two to speak).

A recent look at *Backstage* magazine's calls for writers showed that the one-act play is in high demand. Today's one-act plays are generally no longer than thirty minutes (most are ten to fifteen minutes), and require as few actors as possible. They are generally presented at one-act festivals. Similarly, short screenplays (or "shorts," as they're called) are shot for film festivals. There's rarely much pay for either of these short forms, but it's a feasible way to get your first produced credit. To read *Backstage*'s classifieds on-line, visit http://www.backstage.com/backstage/casting/callboard/writers.jsp. To find calls for screenplays, try Inktip (www.inktip.com), Absolute Markets Premium Edition (www.absolutemarkets.com), and HollywoodLitSales (www.hollywoodlitsales.com).

Novels and Short Stories

If your story requires a lot of backstory, inner dialogue, and subplots, you might just have yourself a novel. Novels are powered by reader's imaginations; your writing must give readers enough credit to allow them to make connections on their own.

Short stories are more than just novels that had to be condensed because the writer ran out of printer paper; they're self-contained stories that don't have to be crammed full of plot. They may be slice-of-life vignettes, single scenes, or they may focus on a particular event, tradition, or relationship. To find markets for short stories, visit Ralan Conley's Webstravaganza at www.ralan.com.

Then there are children's stories, which may be told as picture books, easy readers, middle-grade readers, board books, chapter books, or full-fledged young adult novels. Picture books rely on very few words—they depend on highly visual "scenes" instead.

Don't just decide on your story's form out of habit, or because you feel comfortable in one particular format, or because you're burned out on 90,000-word historical novels and attracted to the short word count of some kids' books. Always be willing to test your limits and expand your scope as a writer. Wanting to write kids' books because they honestly engage you and you think you'd be good at it is one thing. Wanting to write kids' books because you think they're easy—and because they're *only* thirty-two pages—is quite another!

And don't be afraid to switch hands, or even entire teams, halfway through the ball game. One of Patricia Cornwell's first books was a biography of Ruth Bell Graham. Though I'm quite sure Ms. Cornwell applied her unique attention to detail and talent for stringing together evocative phrases to that biography and made it as engaging as any of her subsequent novels, where would the world be without Kay Scarpetta? And where would Kay Scarpetta have come from, if Ms. Cornwell hadn't switched from biographies to thrillers after only a few innings? Imagine if she had switched to children's books instead: "Timmy found a frog in the garden and decided to cut it open and eat its lungs, because he liked the taste of lungs."

▶ PROMPT: Tune into your local country station and listen for an hour. Now turn the radio off and write a country ballad.

Choose the Form Based on What the Story Calls For

I began by calling myself a screenwriter. Later, I defined myself as an article writer. Now, I simply call myself a writer. Period. When a new idea comes to me, I evaluate it to determine which is the most effective way I could tell the story ("Hmm. How about finger puppets?"). I don't stretch an article-length idea into a novel just because I want to call myself a novelist, nor do I think novels are more worthwhile than articles. I don't try to dumb down an honest and evocative young adult novel just because there's a sudden need for middle-grade readers by one of the big publishing houses. I write each piece as it comes, in the form, genre, or page length that it demands ("I'm a 500 word article. Write me. Now!"). I urge you to do the same. You might just find out that a new form suits you just right.

If you're not sure if your story might fit another format, give it a shot, even if you don't plan to finish it. It may give you a new way of looking at your story. Writing a scene or two of your screenplay as a short story may force you to examine your characters' inner dialogue, thereby giving you a better idea of their motivations—or helping you find out they've all got the inner depth of seaweed.

Then again, some forms just plain fit their subject matter. Need evidence? Visit the movie theater once more with me, if you will. We've all seen movies that have been adapted from books, only to fall flat on that big fat silver screen. One of my favorite books in recent years was Helen Fielding's *Bridget Jones's Diary*. I knew from the moment I saw the chapter heading for December's diary entries—*Oh Christ!*—that this was a book I could fall in love with immediately. And fall I did.

I read it aloud to anyone who would listen (and a few who wouldn't—"Back off, lady! I'm in the restroom!") and personally boosted local sales of the book by at least 500 percent. When the paperback came out, it went in every gift bag I gave during that era, and while I was hopeful that a movie adaptation could remain true to the quality of the book, I wasn't quite as sure that it would. And I was right.

When the movie came out, I saw it dutifully, chuckled a few times, but like a returning alumni at my high school reunion noticing my ex-boyfriend's love handles and receding hairline, I couldn't help but be disappointed by missed opportunity and failed expectations. The book was luxurious, big, bold, lavish, and heartfelt. The movie was mere sight gags and food fights. English accents didn't translate into English *charm*, and the witty banter and turn of phrase from the book translated into slick Hollywood one-liners—even if it *was* made in England.

On the other hand, some movies improve on the book. (Stephen King's *Pet Cemetery* comes to mind. So does Tom Clancy's *Hunt for Red October*.) The point is, don't force a square peg into a round hole. If it feels like a screenplay, it's probably a screenplay. If it feels like a novel, it's probably a novel. Forget the trends, forget the two-month-old market report in *Writer's Digest*. Forget what the regulars on your message board for writers are saying is hot.

Stay true to your instinct—your writer's instinct—and the form you're supposed to write in will feel just "write." (I will now duck and put on that raincoat in case the Bad Pun Police find it necessary to hurl rotten tomatoes my way.)

I never thought I'd get writer's block, but it happened last year. After selling nine mainstream historicals, I was dropped by my publisher. I soon drifted away from the everyday habit of sitting down at a computer, and when I did plunk myself down, I couldn't get excited about what I was doing.

One morning I woke up with an idea for incorporating some of my historical research into a time-travel young adult novel (YA), and I was off and running. Before I finished it, I attended a conference for e-writers and talked to a writer who is making not shabby royalty money with an erotica publisher. Once I'd finished the YA, I educated myself about erotica, reworked an old, unsold romance partial, and sent it in. They published it. Third, I decided to write my grandfather's life story, and finally, I wrote a screenplay based on yet another unsold partial.

My advice for outwitting writer's block is to turn things on end. Look at writing possibilities outside what you've done before. Don't retreat from contact with writers or writing organizations. Think outside the box and see if something lights the fire. Sure worked for me.

—Vella Munn, writer

It's Not You, It's Me

17

The Block May be a Symptom of a Larger Problem

And maybe you're just in a funk. Happens to the best of us. There are other possible causes—lifestyle changes, depression, stress, and other problems that may need to be addressed before writing can flow.

Freelance writer April Chase found herself in a spiraling episode of writer's block after she got married. "My first marriage was a disaster!" she says. "I was very young, just starting out, and not yet making much money by writing. I quickly realized my new husband would not and could not hold a job, and that if I had any hope of keeping food on the table by legitimate means, I had better find employment that would pay above the poverty level, fast. So I took a dull but fairly lucrative corporate position and quit writing. Why? Out of disappointment, spite, despair? I really can't define it. Basically, I thought that if I could not write professionally full-time, then I could not be a writer at all."

Every time she tried to write, a wave of sorrow came rushing in. She felt trapped and bitter, and pretty soon, she stopped trying to write altogether—for almost ten years. "Even when that marriage failed," she says, "I was so traumatized by the divorce, the ensuing custody battles, and finally bankruptcy that I still did not write anything. I thought I had forgotten how."

She blew her first opportunity for a reentry into the writing world. She answered an ad in the local paper looking for business journalists and enclosed clips from the "good old days." The editor offered her the job, but when the time came to start planning interviews and actually do the writing, she panicked. "I called up the editor with a lame excuse about a suddenly increased workload at my regular job, blah, blah, sorry, can't do it." She was angry with herself and ashamed that she had backed out, so she almost didn't respond when a second opportunity presented itself a year later.

She read another ad seeking a freelance writer for coverage of a local event and convinced herself to apply. "Once again, to my amazement, I got the job! Somehow, I forced myself through the process—interviewing, writing, editing—thinking all the while that the piece would no doubt be rejected, that I had lost my edge, could no longer write anything worth reading. I waited, then . . . acceptance letter. Then a check! I did it! I am still not sure how I bullied myself into finishing that piece. I tell you, I was in a state of raw panic the whole time. Mainly, it was the thought that it was my last chance; that if I backed out again, no editor would ever even speak to me in the future. But that first article was a hurdle that I had to overcome, and when I did, suddenly it all seemed okay."

Since that time, her writing career has taken off. Every day, she finds it easier to write, query, and follow through. "By forcing myself to just do that first story, despite my fears and certainty I would fail, I vanquished my writer's block."

▶ PROMPT: To help you better understand her, write an acrostic poem using the letters of your main character's name.

The Money Issue

April's feelings are quite common; when money is tight (and let's face it—when isn't it tight?), it sometimes feels trivial and self-serving to write. After all, there are very few writers who earn a substantial living, especially right out of the gates. So it may not be feasible for you to quit your day job and jump right into writing full-time.

That doesn't make you any less of a writer. It only means you're a responsible human being who needs to survive. There's no shame in being a starving writer. It just gets a little uncomfortable at times, particularly when your stomach is growling so loudly it wakes up the neighbors. So most people do what they have to do. Did John Grisham start out as a full-time writer? Heck no. He started as a trial lawyer. And thank goodness. If he hadn't, he might not have had anything to write about!

Don't get yourself into that trap of believing you have to write full-time to be a Real Writer. You can have a full-time job, kids, volunteer work, hobbies, and still be a writer. (Ever heard of Erma Bombeck?) You just have to make the time to write—like during meetings.

But it's just as easy to be blocked when you're busy as it is when you have plenty of time. The block is what it is—you're the only variable.

When Tough Times Fall on You

When you're going through difficult emotional times, such as a divorce, a death in the family, or a health crisis, you may not want to write at all. You have to ask yourself if what you're going through is really writer's block, or if it's just a time in your life when you don't have the concentration required to write.

There's no crime in *not* writing. As we have seen over and over again, putting a little distance between you and your writing can be a good thing, especially when you return to the writing of last week, last month, or even last year with fresh eyes that lead you straight to the weak points, as well as the strong ones, in your story.

But if you're like me, and most writers I know, you can probably tell the difference between a vacation and a block. And when you fall on hard times—physically, emotionally, financially, spiritually—writing is most likely the last thing in the world you want to think about doing.

Even during the toughest times, though, I urge you to use writing as your oasis. Right away, it may be too difficult to write much about the crisis. Only *you* can gauge whether you're ready to tackle it head-on, or whether you'd prefer to distract yourself from it or write things that are only peripherally related to it.

When my grandmother was dying, I needed to find a way to express my love for her. I wasn't sure if she knew who I was anymore when I went to visit her—she didn't nag me once about not being married yet. Although she said "I love you, too" in response to me, it didn't feel like I had—or ever could—say enough.

I went home and knew there were words inside of me that needed to come out. First, I wrote an essay about how my grandparents had met. It turned out to be an inspirational story about faith.

Next, I wrote a poem to my grandmother, as if she weren't dying at all. As if this were just another day and I was letting her know how I felt about her. A novelty gift company bought the poem for use as a wall plaque. She died the next day. The plaque felt like a fitting tribute.

After she died, I was too mixed up inside to write more about her, directly. I kept writing, but now I focused on assignments that would take my mind off of her death. I wrote greeting cards, articles about successful entrepreneurs, and a media kit for AbsoluteWrite.com. There was very little humor in me, so I avoided trying to get ink from that particular dry pen. I used my sentimental pen when writing greeting cards; they weren't deliberately cheerful, but rather pensive and caring.

When I am able to, I will deal with her death in other writings. I haven't been able to bring myself to do it yet, but I plan to learn more about Parkinson's disease and write articles about it. And to write in my journal about what an unafraid, loving, full-of-life woman she always was. Someday, I will want my children to know who their great-grandmother was, and I'd like to write down my favorite stories about her before time wears away at the edges of my memories.

When life gets in the way of your writing, don't beat yourself up if you're not able to summon the energy to write. There may well be a time when you are just too drained to be particularly creative.

▶ PROMPT: Describe your biggest teenage insecurity.

Using the Time for Simpler Tasks

"I rewrite when life circumstances get in the way. That way, I'm still thinking creatively, but I take the pressure off myself to come up with something new and brilliant," says screenwriter Jennifer L. Baum.

Times like these are good for less "straining" writing. Try relying on creative prompts and exercises to come up with new ideas, or take a tip from Jennifer and use this time to rewrite, revise, and proofread. Surely there's something in your repertoire that could use another polish. Take out an older piece of writing, dust it off, and see if you can make it tighter, stronger, and better.

If you have deadlines and can't postpone them, then take it slowly and be easy on yourself. Resign yourself to the fact that this probably won't be the most fun you've ever had while writing, but it's a way to keep moving and show yourself that life goes on.

It may just feel like going through the motions, but it's worthwhile to keep the pen moving as much as you can—and not just rolling it back and forth across your desk. The more you stay away from your writing, the harder it will be to return to it. It's always harder to start a car when the engine's cold. If you can just keep driving a little each day, you'll be in better shape when you're ready to go full force again.

Fortunately (or *un*fortunately, depending on your perspective), recollections have a way of sealing themselves in your long-term memory, like those vacuum-pack bags you see in infomercials at 2 A.M. And while you may not choose to use them right away, and even when you feel like you've lost them forever, they have a funny way of showing up when you least expect them.

Don't worry if you can't trap all those difficult emotions on paper while they're happening. They'll always be there, and you'll always be able to draw them up and turn them over in your mind, examining them from every angle with the wisdom of time coloring them much differently.

Until then, it's important to keep yourself busy, whether rewriting old pieces or writing fluff to keep your mind off of what's happening in your own life.

18

People Who Need People

Finding a Writing Partner

If you're still blocked, consider working with other writers. A writing partner may be just what you need to kick yourself into high gear.

When shopping for a writing partner (aisle 14 at Kmart, next to stationery), ask yourself why you're stuck and try to find a writer who complements your skills. For example, you may be confident in your skills as a researcher, but unsure of how to integrate quotes into your article. You can advertise for a writer who doesn't enjoy interviewing, but is skilled at making transitions and using quotes. Or you may feel strongly about your characters, but less secure about your plotting. Find yourself a writer who knows his or her way around a plot, and you may have yourself a match.

Perhaps you've always wanted to branch out into a particular genre, but just haven't had the courage, or perhaps the know-how. Put out a call for writers in that genre who may be interested in taking on a partner. Maybe you'd love to write a screenplay, and even have a great idea, but even after reading fifteen books on "how to write a screenplay" and the CliffNotes, you still don't feel confident enough to do it for yourself. Advertise for a screenwriter who's long on talent, but temporarily short on story ideas.

Before committing to a writing partnership, it's important to decide how you will work together, and how you will split the work, the credits, the six-pack, and the money, if it comes.

Draw Up a Contract

It's amazing how many friendships crumble when money is involved, so I can't stress enough that you must have a contract. Decide up front whether you're going to do a straight fifty-fifty split, or whether one of the writers will get extra for coming up with the concept, doing more of the preliminary work, selling the work, supplying the coffee, and other tasks like that. Agree to terms before either of you starts working, so neither of you will be competing with the other down the line—if you don't come to an agreement, be aware that the other writer may complete the work alone and market it at the same time you do.

Life is full of nasty little surprises, and the prospect of money seems to bring them out like nothing else. Writing is a business, and you are more than just talented—you are a professional. Treat your writing partnership like you would any other business proposition, and never underestimate how greed can affect a partnership or even a friendship.

Time marches on, and without a binding contract, partners do as well. There's nothing stopping a writing partner from absconding with your work, except perhaps for a nasty and inconclusive "she said, he said" court battle. Don't leave yourself open to the possibility; download a contract from a legitimate and trusted legal or writing Web site, or invest the time and money in having a lawyer do it for you. Chances are your partnership will be a mutually rewarding and beneficial experience, but just like having hurricane insurance in Miami, it never hurts to be safe rather than sorry.

Know Your Partner

Get to know your partner before you commit. Ask to read many of his manuscripts, articles, plays, or books. Know his work ethic, ability to adhere to deadlines, ability to take criticism and editing suggestions ("This sucks. Are you okay with that?"), and ability to "work well with others." Take into account practical considerations as well, such as whether or not your partner has a fax machine and what type of e-mail software he uses. If you're an e-mail-attachment kind of a gal and he's a snail-mail kind of guy, you could run into more than just a few "technical difficulties" along the way. It's best to know about such differences up front than, say, halfway through the project when half of your expense money is going into mailing him overnight packages!

Don't overlook obvious but unspoken clues as well. If you dash off a question at 8 A.M. and he doesn't answer it until 10 P.M., you might want to set up a system of acceptable time lapses between questions and answers. A fourteen-hour time lag might not matter in the beginning of the project, but the closer and closer the deadline looms, hours can become critical, especially fourteen of them.

There are other factors involved here as well. For instance: does he write as fast as you do? Ask. Ask him how many pages he writes in a typical week. Is his grammar atrocious? Is his work ethic good, fair, poor, or indifferent? (You can usually tell based on these questions: how much work has he actually finished versus started, how many times does he typically edit a manuscript, does he consider writing a career or a hobby, and how actively is he marketing his work?)

If all the answers—from both parties—are to your mutual satisfaction, a writing partnership can be a boon to both writers.

▶ PROMPT: You have been chosen as the first writer to go on a space shuttle mission. Describe how you felt during liftoff.

How a Partner Can Help

"Having a partner helped in a lot of ways," says Anne Newgarden. "First of all, it counteracted the avoidance thing. If you make a date to write with a partner, it's harder to break than if you make one with yourself (believe me, I've tried that). Second, it helped with the 'now where do I take the story?' thing: when you hit the wall and can't come up with an idea, chances are your partner will. Third, it *really* helped get past the self-critical stuff that is often at the heart of writer's block. You know, when you get an idea and then there's that little voice in your head that tells you, '*Nah!* That's no good, that'll never work! And you call yourself a writer? Ha!' Your partner (one hopes) would never be as critical of you as you are of yourself. In fact, she's apt to *love* the same idea you might have criticized, unjustly, as being no good. So you get positive reinforcement (and give it in return).

"Working with my partner, Ida, I've finished one feature-length screenplay (which became a semifinalist at the Moondance Film Festival in Colorado this summer, and gleaned us solid interest from an agent), and am now well into the next."

As Anne says, the success of finishing her first screenplay helped her to realize she could cut it as a writer. This spilled over into her solo writing, as well.

Having a writing partner instantly doubles the number of friends you have. Perhaps you are the shy writer type with a close-knit circle of friends who are very similar to you. Well, your writing partner may be the popular extrovert writer with lots of connections, acquaintances, and contacts. Not only does this provide for ample life lessons, but you'll be on the receiving end of quite a bit of networking, which could come in handy when it comes time for publication, marketing, and promotion.

It also doesn't hurt when a less-experienced writer with fewer credits attaches himself to a more experienced writer with lots of publishing credits. This symbiotic relationship may seem to help the newbie writer more, but it can be mutually beneficial when the less-experienced writer offers to take on more of the writing, researching, or interviewing duties in exchange for the contacts and possible name recognition the more published writer (who will be out playing golf) may bring to the partnership.

Where to Find a Partner

If you don't already have lots of writing friends, it couldn't be simpler to meet them. Hop on-line and visit writer hangouts. Here are a few of the best:

Absolute Write Water Cooler (http://pub43.ezboard.com/babsolutewrite): There's a board specifically for critiques and writing partners. Just log on and advertise your desire for a partner.

Writers Write Message Boards (http://www.writerswrite.com/messages/): There are boards here for all different genres. Introduce yourself and find someone who works in yours.

Zoetrope (http://www.zoetrope.com): For screenplays, novellas, short stories, flash fiction, and poetry. This is a spot where you can workshop your writing (give and receive critiques), as well as meet other writers on the message boards and in the chat room.

Momwriters (http://groups.yahoo.com/group/momwriters/): An e-mail Listserv where you can meet other writers who "face the unique challenges of writing with children underfoot."

iVillage Readers and Writers Message Boards (http://www.ivillage.com/books/boards): Women's message boards on topics ranging from fiction writing to getting published. Meet friendly writers and ask questions here.

Script Secrets (http://pub18.ezboard.com/bscriptsecrets): Find your screenwriting partner at this message board.

Writing Groups

If working with a partner isn't for you, then consider joining a writing group where you can bounce ideas off people and get feedback. Writing groups can offer all of the benefits of having a writing partner without many of the legal hassles. For instance, members of a writing group can often critique each other's writing with beneficial advice. New writers bring new enthusiasm, old writers bring experience and life lessons. Both are advantageous to the other party.

Writing groups also offer networking opportunities and often engage in group promotions for those writers whose work has been published and need a little extra help in the grassroots promotional department. Try these Web sites for on-line writing communities:

Coffeehouse for Writers (www.coffeehouseforwriters.com): Offers active e-mail Listservs for writers, moderated critique groups (there is usually a waiting list), and writing exercises.

Arcanum Café (www.arcanumcafe.com/community): Active message boards for poets. You can discuss the writing life or get critiques of your poetry.

One of Us (www.oneofus.co.uk): Creative writing workshop and discussion list for amateur and professional writers.

Critters Workshop (www.critters.org): A 3,000-member workshop and critique group for science fiction, fantasy, and horror writers.

Red Pencil (www.redpencil.net): Fiction, nonfiction, and poetry are all welcome here. You can post your writing for feedback and comment on other people's writing.

▶ PROMPT: Write a letter to your favorite author.

Dealing with Unhelpful Feedback

When gathering feedback about your work, be sure to wear your protective shield—the one that protects you from unhelpful criticism and those who would have you change your story to fit their voices. Linda Adams, cowriter of an upcoming women's Civil War thriller, says, "I didn't have confidence in my own writing abilities. I had to show my work to others, watch to see if they laughed or smiled or frowned or whatever. Then they made comments. I immediately rushed back to make changes based on their comments—even if I didn't think the changes were right. Because I didn't have confidence in my own abilities, I figured they must be right. So I made the changes, and suddenly the stories weren't what I originally intended anymore."

This sent her straight to writer's block prison for two years. Finally, she broke the block by writing fan fiction about the 1960s science fiction television series *Voyage to the Bottom of the Sea*. "It was nice and safe," she says. "I could write, it would get published, and everyone liked it. No one came back and told me they didn't understand something. Rather, they were grateful—even excited—to read some new adventures of the characters."

She came to understand that she couldn't let her confidence as a writer come from outside sources. She had to know that her writing was good, not rely on having others tell her so. "Then, one day, I got a story published. I sent it to one of the people I'd relied on for their opinion. He looked at it and said, 'I don't get it.' It was then I realized the people I'd been asking for help really didn't know good fiction from a tree stump."

19

Take a Little Trip

Visiting the Megabookstore

If all else fails and you still find yourself in the quill-pen quag-mire of writer's block, it's time to take a little trip. No, put down those pills. Just save whatever you're working on, even if it's a blank document, shut down your computer, put on some clothes (for those of you who take that "I work in my boxer shorts" stereotype literally), grab the car keys, and head off to the nearest megabookstore.

Yes, I said *mega*bookstore.

Avoid the homey, cutesy, mom-and-pop bookstore you nor-mally frequent to "stick it to the man" and head to the biggest, gaudiest, name-brandiest chain bookstore you can find. You may have to come down off of your mountain top or, good grief, get on the freeway at rush hour. Of course, at the rate these bookstores are expanding to accommodate the latest genre (Jewish romantic horror comedy), you could just sit tight for a week and wait for the building to come to you.

Now take a few deep breaths and enter this shrine to all things commercial. Give yourself a few hours to worship there like the rest of the consumers who put buying books right up there with toothpaste or shampoo. While you're at it, treat yourself to a frozen cappuccino creation and a biscotti. Just give yourself ample cruising time and then, well, start cruising through the endless aisles of mass-market paperbacks, oversized coffee-table books, and undersized gift books. Hope you brought a compass.

Drop In on Your Writing Family

If you're blocked while writing a novel, check out the latest best-sellers. Avoid sneering at the latest life-size glamour shot of Danielle Steel and objectively study the spines and then the front and back covers of the books you find there. What are people reading? What do all the books have in common? What are the wild cards? Who are the biggest names? Who are the new names? Who are the old standbys?

Pick up the megabookstore's free in-store newspaper—they all publish one these days—and read it from cover to cover while you lounge in the café. (They all have one of those, too.) Read the summaries, the reviews, the blurbs, even the ads. Get a feel for what's going on in the market these days, for what's changed, and for what's still the same. Universal. Timeless. Classic.

If you're writing a nonfiction fitness book, wander over to the Health and Beauty aisle and do the same thing. Ditto for magazine articles, kids' books, thrillers, romances, computer books, greeting cards, and so on.

Where's Your Book?

Now—*stop*. Right where you are. Standing. Sitting. Kneeling. Making gagging noises. And look around. See the young couple taking the latest impotency quiz in *Cosmo*. Smile at the teenagers giggling over *The Joy of Sex*. Arch your eyebrows at the Goth babe preparing to shoplift a copy of *Necronomicon*. Witness the Tom Clancy wannabe in his spy glasses and turtleneck.

Then picture yourself—or more accurately—picture your novel, your diet book, your magazine article, or your picture book for disabled kids. Whatever your genre, where would it be on the shelf? *Why* would someone read it? How *many* people would read it? What would be special about it? What is it lacking? What does it already have that makes it stand out?

Is there a book currently out there that might compete with it? Is it filling a niche that's yet to be filled? Is it cliché or revolutionary? Is it timely or classic? Would the Goth babe like it? How about the teenagers? The Tom Clancy wannabe? Why? Why not?

▶ PROMPT: Pretend you've just checked into a hotel room, only to hear the unmistakable sounds of lovemaking in the next room. Who are the two characters, and what are they doing there?

The Book Business

Realize, fully and perhaps for the very first time, that writing is a business. That it's not all fairy tales and ogres, dreams coming true, and cups of piping hot tea between Dorothy Parker and Virginia Woolf. Despite what your uncle *still* says about you "getting a real job" or the drawer in your filing cabinet overflowing with rejection letters, you are part of an amazing and awe-inspiring business that brings joy, education, inspiration, and information into the lives of hundreds of thousands of people every single day.

Writers often take their work far too emotionally and as such get frustrated by the business aspect of publishing. They insulate themselves with fantasy and fancy, forgetting that somewhere out there, someone has to actually *sell* their book to customers. And not just one, but one thousand, one hundred thousand or more. Publishers are not the bad guys any more than are editors or the folks in book design or marketing. These are simply people trying to make a living in the same business as you are.

The fact that they sell words, including *your* words someday, with any luck, doesn't make them different from the kind of people who sell soap, towels, or sunscreen. Publishers are in the business of making money; they just happen to make money on words. Thousands of them if they're magazine publishers, tens of thousands of them if they're in the book business.

I know this is a hard exercise, perhaps the hardest one in this book. Many writers have a love-hate relationship with the glitzy, commercial, plastic gloss of the megabookstores, where only the strong survive and the rest get budget prices in the bargain bins before being shoved into a big cardboard box and returned to the disappointed publisher whence they came (they don't even give the authors the option to have the books cremated). On the one hand, a bookstore offers us the chance to be surrounded by the words, the authors, the books that we love so very much. On the other, few of us can find our own books there. It's frustrating, it's unfair, it's degrading, and it breeds professional jealousy in a profession that should know—and do—better.

Most of us have been writing since we were children, and those of us who weren't early starters were at least dreaming of writing since we were children. This fact alone makes the act of writing loaded with excess personal baggage and at the very least an extremely emotional act.

We've all succumbed to the fantasy and have been found guilty of interviewing ourselves about the symbolism of our setting, the eloquence of our language, the three-dimensionality of our characters. We've all donned smoking jackets and popped a pipe, even if it was just a corncob version, into our mouths and struck our Hugh Hefner pose. We've all dreamed the dream, but it's only a rare few who have actually *lived* it.

Yet standing in a crowded bookstore watching customers engage in the commerce of words should make it all too clear that you are entering into a business relationship, no matter how emotionally attached you are to your own lovely words.

Perhaps, just by realizing this, it will make you crash through your writer's block as soon as you get home. If not, perhaps drawing a moustache on Danielle Steele's latest glamour shot will.

20

The $6 Solution: Six Items to Help You Beat Writer's Block

Visiting the Dollar Store

Writers have a tendency to overthink things. And, ironically, when a writer gets writer's block, he doesn't think less—he thinks more!

The thinking fills his head day and night, night and day. It crowds out his imagination, his inspiration, his motivation. It invades any new ideas for writing he may have, and banishes the old. The thinking overtakes the writing until the writer is thinking about so much more, he writes less and less and less.

But sometimes, less *is* more. Sometimes, writers need to think less—and *do* more. Maybe visiting your local library or bookstore won't be the key that unlocks your block. Maybe feng shui won't do it either (but feel free to keep pushing the furniture around—it's good exercise). Perhaps outwitting your writer's block can be as simple as moseying on down to your local dollar store and stocking up on the following six items:

A Calendar

Dollar stores specialize in inexpensive calendars—and so should every writer. I have four or five calendars going at any one time in a given year. Some fit in my backpack, some hang on the wall, one resides in the folder for my taxes, the ugly ones become gifts for relatives I can't stand, and on and on it goes. One is for my finances: who paid what for which and when did they do it? One is for deadlines: what's due when and how long is it supposed to be and why? One is for submissions: what did I send to whom and when? And so on.

This is a different kind of therapy from the one in this book that uses a day planner. This time, I want you to pick a dollar store calendar; your choice—horses, clowns, butterflies, frogs, or daisies on the front—and use it to outwit your writer's block. Use it any way you wish. You can fill in the blanks with the various writing exercises you're using to beat that nasty block. (December 26: reasons to buy Aunt Ethel an even uglier calendar next year as revenge for the eggnog you think she intentionally poisoned.) You can fill it with page numbers from this book that were particularly helpful or illuminating. You can fill it with memorable dates that produced outpourings of magnificent writing. You can use it for triumphs and setbacks, wishes and dreams, rejections and acceptances.

The point is to *use* it, and use it often. Not only might this practice help you to get better organized, but it will hopefully help you begin to express yourself more—as well as more *often*. The simple act of putting pen or pencil to paper, even if it is to fill in those thirty monthly squares, is an extremely effective tool for beating back the beast of blockage.

It might also help to track the block. For instance, if you are a writer who gets blocked more than once a month, develop a simple code for those days when you feel blocked. A big, black "B," perhaps. Or a green one with slime oozing off of it. As the year progresses, make it a habit to look over the past months and check to see where those Bs are most likely to fall. Always during the first week of the month? How about the last? Every third Wednesday? Holidays? Birthdays? Anniversaries? On the weekend? Along with the Monday blues?

Knowing when you have a tendency to get blocked might just help you stave off your next block. Or if dwelling on when you are blocked becomes a preoccupation, accentuate the positive and draw big yellow smiley faces in the days when you're *not* blocked. Litter the days and weeks of each month with enough smiley faces and you may just like looking at them so much that you decide you'll never allow yourself to get blocked again. Either that or they'll drive you completely insane.

Writing is a habit. Whether we write down a schedule, or just keep it tacked to the back of our mind (warning: pushing the tack in hurts like heck), most of us stick to one. Schedules, routines, and habits may seem restricting, but in reality they provide a helpful framework in which the writer can feel free to let herself go, throw off the reins, and write with the wind.

The worst part about being blocked is that you're messing with your habit. Use the calendar as a tool to get back into the swing of writing—and a way to remember your stepmother's birthday!

▶ PROMPT: Describe each of the items you might put into a gift bag—and why—for your ex-spouse or lover.

A (Really Neat) Pen

Just like your (really ugly) notebook, there's something to be said about a (really neat) pen. (Or a whole bunch of really neat pens.) Especially for a writer. Long before most of us could afford—or even reach—a Smith Corona or, for those of us lucky enough to be born in the '80s, a Macintosh or IBM keyboard, we started with a pen. Or pencils. Or crayons. Or chalk. Or charcoal. But mostly, a pen. (We kept eating the crayons.)

A pen was more dignified than a pencil. More grown-up. More "writerly." It didn't need to be sharpened like a pencil, wouldn't melt in your hand like some crayons, and took a really long time to run out of ink.

Some were castoffs from mom's purse, dad's office, a bigger sibling's backpack, the doctor's office, or the bank (you've still got the chain that used to attach it to the counter). We sometimes branched out from the strangle hold of blue and black ink and explored different colors for different emotions or different genres: red ink for love poems, green ink for keeping track of all the money we'd make as a famous writer some day, blue ink for sad stories, and so on. Our notebooks, diaries, and journals filled with the rainbow colors of idealism, hope, and our limitless imagination. As kids, we were suckers for neat pens.

So where did that feeling go, anyway? When did we stop using ink from all the colors of the rainbow? When did we quit being pen connoisseurs? And when, for that matter, did we stop using pens that looked like other, well, *things*? Trolls. Barbie dolls. Surfboards. Sunflowers. Rocket ships. On a recent trip to Disney World, every gift shop I visited had pens topped with Mickey ears, or Donald's beak, or Pluto's nose, or Minnie's bow. "What a great idea," I thought.

How magical. How fun! How inspiring . . .

But you don't have to spend eight dollars on a Mickey Mouse or Donald Duck pen like I did. (Sucker!) You can learn from my experience and simply head to the dollar store instead. Here you'll find pens of all colors, shapes, and sizes.

After all, the trick is to outwit your writer's block, not just your checkbook. Start using a diary again, and write in it only with your new special pen. Never use your special pen for daily chores, like signing your kids' report cards or filling out the grocery list. It's a special pen, just for writing. Use it to capture the fun and magic and hope and dreams you had as a kid. Use it to tap into your inner child. Use it to add a little much-needed color or fun or whimsy to your writing day. Don't let writer's block—or even being an adult—rob you of that enthusiasm of youth.

Let your special pen be a link to your past, and write away.

A Mascot

Perhaps what you *really* need to help you through your current state of writer's block is a pal—an inanimate object designed to cheer you on, help you through your frustration, make you smile, sit there quietly, and never, *ever* ask a silly question like, "Aren't you done writing that yet?!"

A mascot, if you will.

And there's no better place to pick up an inexpensive mascot than the dollar store. From rubber dinosaurs to stuffed teddy bears, from plastic aliens to bobblehead dogs, you'll find a cornucopia of fake friends to take home and nurture. (Or is it the other way around?) Maybe your mascot takes on the form of a colorful squeezie ball that gets manhandled when your writer's block gets the worst of you. Or perhaps you need a snuggly doll to hold and caress when you can't seem to get unblocked. Maybe you need a giant-sized grasshopper to revitalize your writing sessions. Or a field of green army men surrounding your computer monitor.

Take your time and choose your dollar store mascot wisely. After all, depending on how long this case of writer's block decides to stick around, you could be seeing a whole lot of each other in the coming weeks.

Perhaps your mascot doesn't even come from the toy aisle. Perhaps it's a baby bottle, as you try to complete the daunting task of writing a book for expectant mothers (goodness knows what you'll buy when you get to the breast-feeding section). Maybe it's a hula hoop, to help inspire you to complete that chronology of the '50s you keep putting off. Maybe it's a pair of gloves or a spatula.

Whatever your choice, treat your mascot well and he'll do the same.

Bubbles

Don't laugh. Oh, fine, laugh if you must. Blowing bubbles is a long-forgotten art and one of the cheapest cures for writer's block I've ever come across. Not only that, but if you buy them at the dollar store, you can get a whole year's supply for less than a buck.

I discovered this simple trick recently at a relative's wedding. Now that rice is thought to be dangerous to birds (which is a myth, by the way) and bird seed is passé, bubbles are the next great thing for sending off the lucky couple to their can-adorned limousine. (Until that, too, becomes passé, of course.) Snagging a couple of extra bottles from the overflowing woven baskets by the door, I planned on taking them home as souvenirs of the lucky couple's special day.

However, I soon found them to be a welcome addition to my daily writing chores as well. One morning, while I was waiting for my computer to boot up—it takes a week these days—I idly blew a few wands full of bubbles from the miniature blowers (they're shaped like tiny champagne bottles—too cute) I'd snagged at the wedding. To my delight, they cascaded through-out my home office like wet fairy dust, covering my work space with a sparkling array of whimsy that rejuvenated my soul until I slipped on the greasy section of the floor where all the bubbles had landed.

I was hooked. Ever since I got the cast off my arm, I've been blowing bubbles in my office for good luck. Some days, if I'm having a serious problem with a particular scene, I'll open the page on my monitor and blow bubbles in its direction. Other times, if I'm sending off a particularly important query letter, book proposal, or manuscript, I'll blow a wand full of crystal-clear bubbles to float and then descend upon my 9-by-12-inch envelopes. Other times I just blow a dozen or so bubbles in the general direction of my desk to bring a smile to my face—and inspiration to my soul.

And, while I still get rejected, dejected, and discouraged, a quick blow of bubbles never fails to put me in a smiling—and often a writing—mood. Perhaps they'll do the same for you.

▶ PROMPT: Are your grandparents still alive? If so, interview one or both of them for a profile of their lives. If not, write your own version.

A Snack

Ever heard the saying "Feed a cold, starve a fever"? Why shouldn't the same be said for writer's block? While I certainly don't suggest eating yourself out of house and home, there's nothing wrong with giving yourself a little treat now and then, and there's no better place to get treats (and a whole lot of 'em) than the dollar store.

Not only will you find wonderful bargains, such as 4,000 Tootsie Rolls for a buck, but you'll often run across treats you haven't seen since childhood. Like Pop Rocks, Lemonheads, Mary Janes, Hot Tamales, Necco Wafers, those wax bottles filled with sugary colored water, and my all-time favorite, Pixie Sticks! All in boxes too big to fit in your shopping cart. Just make sure the use-by dates aren't in Roman numerals.

Use these rarified treats systematically to sabotage your writer's block. Dole out the treats by the chapter, by the page, by the paragraph, or, if you've got a sweltering metabolism like mine, by the sentence.

If your health, your teeth, or even your weight is concerned, the treats don't even have to be candy. You might buy yourself stickers. They're full of fiber, and virtually fat free! But seriously, folks, I have an author acquaintance who treats herself to a sticker on the page whenever she's happy with her writing, just like her second-grade teacher would do. My fiancé, Anthony, teaches music lessons, and one day, after a particularly good private lesson, his nine-year-old student rewarded *him* by placing a sticker on Anthony's music case. How's that for a lesson?

Buy a 500-piece puzzle and give yourself a break after each writing triumph to find where one piece goes. Buy a boomerang and allow yourself time per word to go throw it around in the front yard. (If it doesn't come back, they've probably sold you a stick.)

Slowly, as your writer's block fades into your not-too-distant past, wean yourself off of this artificial high and march back up the scales. If you formerly rewarded yourself with a Lemonhead per sentence, kick it up to one Lemonhead per paragraph. Then, the next day, per page. And so on.

So, okay, you'll have high blood sugar—but at least you'll be writing!

A Book of Word Searches

Word searches may be the most underrated—and inexpensive—tool in the medicine cabinet we're designing to outwit your current case of writer's block. Most dollar stores offer numerous volumes and genres of word searches, from celebrity names to sports, from travel to history, and often they're even two for one. Invest in one (or two or three or four) and take some time to really delve into solving the first few puzzles that catch your eye.

Once they're complete, give yourself an assignment. Can't think of one yourself? Okay, I'll give you one instead: use each and every word you discovered inside the wordfind in a poem, article, or short story. Keep the title from the wordfind itself. They're often rather clever (for a fifty-cent book anyway), like "Dialing for Dollars" or "Pinch Hitter." When you're through using all of the words you found (are you sure you used them *all*?) staple your story to the back of the word search you used to complete it.

Not only will this give you a sense of accomplishment (not too many people use the word "plague" in a love poem), but most likely, before the whole book is through—your writer's block will be as well.

Make a game of it and complete one word-search story a day, or a week, or a month. Whatever your pace, always keep a few books worth of wordfinds handy and continue to use this writing assignment long after your writer's block has vanished, along with the person you gave the poem to.

Creativity is the key when fighting—and especially beating—writer's block, and mind games like this one are the lifeblood of creativity. Any form of therapy such as this—quick, easy, fun, creative, imaginative, did I say "fun"?—can be used again and again as you mature and develop as a writer.

The key to making writer's block appear less and less in your life is practicing good writing habits that employ creativity, sensitivity, imagination, and good old-fashioned fun. The less drudgery your writing schedule contains, the less opportunity writer's block has to rear its ugly head and derail your writing flow.

Cultivate word games like this. Use them often. Use them well. And the more you do, the less likely you are to suffer from writer's block.

I am so full of ideas I can burst at any time! The dashboard of my car was usually a display of my week. I had notes posted everywhere, and I carried paper, pens, and Scotch tape with me at all times.

I began to realize this year that my habit of writing everything down in the car was dangerous. Oftentimes, you could see me with a piece of paper spread out across the steering wheel of my car, scribbling down my ideas while my eyes jumped from road to paper and back to road.

So for Christmas, I bought myself a neat little gadget: a tiny tape recorder. In these times, when so many people drive and talk on their cell phones at the same time, I fit right in. No one can tell that I am talking to a recorder instead of a phone. For someone who is a tad bit clutter-brained, this might be the perfect solution.

—Heide A. W. Kaminski, freelance writer

21

Let the Market Be Your Guide

Pick a Department, Any Department

Maybe you're not buying into this "writing-as-its-own-reward" concept and you're in need of more of an incentive than a completed manuscript or yet another Letter-to-the-Editor credit.

We've already talked about contests and the positive effect they may have on overcoming your writer's block, but perhaps you need something a little less chancy, a little more concrete. Then it's time to let the markets guide you.

Some magazines, e-zines, newspapers, and journals put out very detailed writers' guidelines. I want you to track down the guidelines for a market you enjoy reading. Now look specifically for information about regular columns (or departments) that are not staff written. If you don't find this information in the guidelines, then figure it out on your own. Look at three recent issues of your favorite magazine and find out which pages carry the same title each week. (Yes, I want you to complete this exercise even if you have no desire to ever write for magazines. Stretch those literary muscles.)

For example, *Woman's Day* runs certain consistent features in each issue. The "How-To" page contains short, informational tidbits about a wide variety of subjects. The "Neighbors" page is where readers tell stories about neighbors who have gone above and beyond the call of duty. "Happy Endings" is a back-page essay that—well, has a happy ending. "Words of Wisdom" is also an essay page that tells of a lesson learned. "Your Health" is for short news, studies, and warnings that are health related. "Kid's Day" is for unusual parenting tips.

What I want you to do is to pick one department and give yourself an assignment based on what you read. If your aim is to be published, try to find a topic that isn't unique to the magazine so that it can be sold elsewhere if that magazine rejects it. You might pick "Happy Endings," for example. If *Woman's Day* turns it down, you can find plenty of other magazines that look for feel-good stories.

So, give yourself a word count based on the length that appears in the magazine, and set a deadline. Surely, you've had something go right in your life once or twice. There was that time the ice-cream man let you get away with being a nickel short, if nothing else.

Now that your teachers are (presumably) out of your life, it's time to give yourself homework and to evaluate it accordingly. Make this your homework and see how you do with it. Instead of starting from scratch every time and trying to brainstorm a new topic, let the market do a little of the work for you by writing according to its established topics.

▶ PROMPT: Pick two of your favorite characters from a television series you remember from your youth. Now write yourself a page of dialogue.

Get Anthologized

Have you ever thought about being anthologized?

Anthologies are the ultimate gift book, airport bookstore purchase, and holiday stocking stuffer. From *Chicken Soup for the Grandmother's Soul* (HCI) to *Stories for an Extreme Teen Heart* (Multnomah Publishers), they reach every population and span every book budget. Their trade paperback size makes them easy reading for young and old alike, and their $10 price range makes them affordable gifts or treasured keepsakes, depending on your budget.

Often mocked by the literary elite, these heartwarming gift books nonetheless top the best-seller lists at every major bookstore chain in the country, consistently outselling nonfiction titles by some of today's hottest and most respected authors. So, who writes all those stories?

How does a 21-year-old creative writing major get to put "best-selling author" on her résumé? How does an ex-football coach add three, four, or even more books on the shelf next to his dozens of championship trophies? How does a retired engineer who's never taken a journalism course wind up writing for such Madison Avenue publishers as William Morrow, Harper-Collins, and New World Library?

Simple: They sleep around.

No, no, that's not it at all. They get *anthologized!*

I'm a confirmed anthology hound and use every opportunity I can to appear in as many anthologies as possible. It's not for the ego, and it's certainly not for the money, but I find the subject matter of most of them heartwarming—and how cool is it to be able to give someone a book as a gift, only to have them discover that you wrote a story about them inside?

When I wrote a letter for *Love Letters of a Lifetime,* I expected it to be one heck of a Valentine's Day gift for Anthony. But it snowballed—the anthology was the basis for a television special and we were invited to appear. Then we began fielding calls from talk shows and movie producers who were interested in our love story. All because I spent an hour or so composing a sweet letter for inclusion in an anthology.

Chicken Soup for the Soul. A Gift of Miracles. Chocolate for a Woman's Heart. God Allows U-Turns. A Cup of Comfort. Such inspirational, heartwarming—not to mention best-selling—titles become instant household words to a reading public that crosses age, racial, economic, and gender boundaries.

The instant cache of appearing in a best-selling anthology gives a budding freelance writer, would-be journalist, or future author almost overnight credibility. Adding *Chicken Soup for the Soul* to a résumé that formally contained little more than "letter to the editor, *Walnut Grove Times*" is a meteoric boost.

Likewise, the potential exposure for one's writing career can be unparalleled on the whirlwind anthology publicity circuit. Popular and profitable anthologies such as *A Cup of Comfort* often invite contributors to participate in readings and signings at bookstores around the country. Who knows how many bookstore managers and audience members can become your very own personal writing network?

More important, the mere act of trying to get anthologized might be your ticket out of writer's block. Think about it. *Chicken Soup for the Soul,* regardless of what you think of the writing inside or their franchising of the written word, has books for every race, creed, gender, profession, or sport known to man. *Chicken Soup for the Irish Soul. Chicken Soup for the Golfer's Soul. Chicken Soup for the Grandmother's Soul.* Why, there's even a *Chicken Soup for the Writer's Soul!*

With all those titles running around out there, and more (and more and more and more and more) coming out each year, there's bound to be a *Chicken Soup* book, published or forthcoming, that's right up your alley.

So why not write a story for one? This therapy has two options: one for those who want to turn their writer's block into cash (the folks at *Chicken Soup* currently pay $300 for a story), and one for those who just want to break the chains of writer's block and return to their computer keyboard unshackled by the bonds of doubt, frustration, and worry.

For option one, check out the links at www.absolutewrite.com/freelance_writing/anthologies.htm. That's where I place links to anthologies' calls for submissions. You'll find markets you're familiar with, and some you've never seen before (ever heard of *Chalkdust on the Sleeve of My Soul?* I thought not). On each Web site linked, you'll find guidelines and, usually, sample stories.

Not only will the act of writing a story for an anthology help you in itself, but going through the process of researching the site, the series, and other sample stories might just kick your brain into overdrive and spur on a writing spell unparalleled in your own personal history. When you're done, spend some extra time refining and rewriting it, just to make sure your writer's block has taken a permanent vacation. Then send it off. Who knows? It might even be accepted.

For option number two, you don't have to do as much research. You can use an existing or even a forthcoming anthology title or simply make one up.

This might be the funnier option of the two, although you might have a slightly smaller chance of getting published. Imagine the titles you could come up with: *Chicken Soup for the Gilligan's Island Fan's Soul, Chocolate for Left-Handed Breast-Feeding*

Women, A Cup of Comfort for Laid-Off Dot-Commers, God Allows U-Turns for Old Hippies.
Let your imagination run wild and write, write, write. Write one story. Write two stories. Write a whole collection of your stories.

▶ PROMPT: Describe a time when you witnessed someone doing something selfless or brave.

Happy Holidays

Holidays aren't just for Santa and the Easter Bunny anymore. Try President's Day, Valentine's Day, Fourth of July, Halloween, Samhain, Thanksgiving, Arbor Day, Hanukkah, Kwanzaa, New Year's Eve, World Salami Appreciation Day, and who can forget good old St. Patrick's Day?

While most of these "greeting card" holidays are just excuses for a day off to our nonwriting neighbors, you can be inspired to write every day of the year if you take advantage of the holidays.

Don't let your writer's block make you dwell on the negative all year long; simply look up and down the nearest aisle of greeting cards and accentuate the positive. Use the seasons, but more importantly the holidays, to outwit your writer's block 365 days a year.

Don't sit at home dwelling on why you don't have a date for Valentine's Day—or why your hubby only shows up with flowers or candy and not *both*! Use this unhappy holiday experience to your advantage. Capitalize on it. Write a story about it. Or fill a plethora of imaginary greeting cards with holiday slogans you'd like to see, such as "Roses are red, violets are blue, I just filled the holes in your bowling ball with Super Glue," or even imaginary recipients, like "To The New Guy with the Cute Butt in

Marketing." Write Valentine's cards to ex-boyfriends, future ex-boyfriends, or boyfriends you had—or wanted to have—in third grade. Write a romance novel about the perfect boyfriend, or the boyfriend who's perfectly sinful.

Come that chocolaty holiday known as Easter, write a kid's book about the Easter Bunny. Or the Easter Bunny's evil twin, Money Bunny. Write about what it feels like to be a hard-boiled egg, or a tablet of food coloring, or a chocolate bunny's ears. Write about the day the jelly beans all went sour, or invent an imaginary array of jelly beans that taste like vegetables.

Each holiday make a point of writing something themed to that occasion. Maybe an Arbor Day article about the rain forests, maybe a Columbus Day travelogue. If you like writing for periodicals, you're in for a treat with this exercise; most magazines, newspapers, and even literary journals look for seasonal and holiday-related stories. Just be aware of lead times; most magazines will need to see your query letter about six months before the holiday month. (Yes, it really is Christmas in July.) And, obviously, holidays are quintessential for greeting-card writers. But, again, you can choose to write this type of material to sell, to record traditions for future generations, or just to enjoy yourself.

And don't feel embarrassed if you're excited about writing the diary of Mrs. Claus—half the battle of outwitting writer's block is getting excited about writing again, no matter what the source of inspiration.

If the holidays do that for you, all the better.

22

Plagiarism is Good?!

Getting Started by Ripping Off Another Writer

I have a new mantra for you: Plagiarism is good.

What's that you say? An author is suggesting that we go out and copy other people's ideas and pass them off as our own? That we publish a 300-page cheat sheet and hope nobody—least of all the author we ripped off—notices? Is *that* her answer to overcoming writer's block?

And where do I sign up?

First, let me explain myself. As someone who makes her living from the written word, I'd be the last person to suggest you pass off someone else's writing as your own, no matter how good it is—or how much Random House offers you! (How much *are* they offering you, anyway?)

However, in my experience, temporarily "lifting" a few fine paragraphs from your favorite book or author is a great way to smooth out the transition from blocked to overflowing. And I'm not alone. You may remember this unique and effective technique from the blockbuster movie *Finding Forrester*.

When main character, Jamal, who is perhaps Hollywood's first treatment of a fleshed-out character who just happens to be suffering from writer's block, can't seem to get started on his paper for a very tony prep school, that lovable Forrester (Sean Connery) lends him one of his own papers just to give him a head start. A little push in the right direction.

Advised to just start hitting the keyboard and hitting it while copying the first few paragraphs of Forrester's well-written article, Jamal soon finds himself typing away, fueled by his own steam. While using plagiarized words to prime his creative pump, Jamal soon finds himself inspired enough to begin putting down his own words.

The technique works so well that Jamal is off and flying, his own words spilling over the page as the simple act of typing slowly but surely converts into the currency of *writing*. Not just one word, or one sentence, or one page, but page after page after page.

So, if it works in the movies, why wouldn't it work for you? Often, blocked writers find themselves so paralyzed with dread of the entire writing process that it takes on physical manifestations as well. The fear of not being able to write leapfrogs into a fear of typing as well. The logic goes like this: "I'm afraid I'll never be able to write another word. Where do I write? The computer. So, if I don't go near the computer, I won't be affected. Right?? I'd better get a Playstation so I can still play computer games."

Naturally, the first step to curing this particular strain of writer's block, commonly referred to in the industry as "Fear and Loathing in Smith Corona," is to lead oneself, slowly but surely, back to the typewriter or keyboard. And how better to accomplish that tricky feat than to simply type? And type. And type and type and type.

▶ PROMPT: Your preteen daughter wants you to tell her how she'll know when she's in love. What do you tell her?

Typing Therapy

Go grab your favorite paperback or hardcover. Now open it up. Anywhere. Start at the beginning of page 1, or in the middle of page 101. Flip the pages like a deck of cards and start wherever your finger lands. Doesn't matter, you couldn't care less. The trick is to rehabilitate your fingers to get back in typing mode, and if this method of tricking them works, then so much the better for you and your writing career. After all, your fingers don't know any better. The brain is the mastermind behind this whole writer's block operation.

Now, start typing. Don't try to edit said best-selling author, no matter how much he or she might need it. Don't get bogged down in grammatical errors and typos, fonts or serifs, or antonyms or synonyms. Don't worry about the type size or the spacing or indents or any of that stuff. Just start typing.

Doesn't matter if it's a sex scene, the dramatic climax, or the middle of a lackluster comedy bit. Doesn't matter if the dialect is syrupy Southerner or uptight Londoner. Type the words that come, *as* they come, and let the feeling take you away, farther and farther from the clinging grasp of your needy little case of writer's block.

Type until you're lost in the story, until you don't know where you are, until the room has fallen away and the curtains could be in flames for all you care. Type until you've filled a few paragraphs or more, then put the curtains out. Consider this "typing therapy."

Now, take a deep breath. Blink your tired eyes. Crack, crick, stretch, and bend your fingers. Count to ten, using your freshly-bent fingers if necessary. Then print it all out.

A Body in Motion Tends to Stay in Motion

Now read what you typed. Read it word for word, typos, plagiarism, funky font, small type size, places where you acCIDEN-

TALLY HIT THE CAPS LOCK key and all. Devour it and smile. Now take up where you left off. Keep writing. Keep typing. Continue the story.

Only this time, shut the book. Put it away. Bury it, if you have to. Whatever you do, this time around, *don't* copy. Don't plagiarize. Don't just type, but *write!* This time I want you to write with your own words, your own phrases, your own ideas.

Maybe what you've written from the author's version ended with a cliffhanger, maybe it ended midsentence, maybe it was a chapter break, maybe it was just the copyright symbol. Doesn't matter. Simply write what happens next. Kill the main character off, or bring her back to life. Rescue the damsel in distress, or ask the coffee shop waitress out to a movie and dinner. Sneak in some dragons, jazz up the joint, throw in a few curse words just for spice.

The point is, it's up to *you.*

Whatever you do, don't try to recreate the author's style. Don't use her flowery language if yours is sparser and more evocative. Don't try to copy his hip, fluent, staccato riffs if your style is quieter, more cunning, and more calculating. Just start where he or she left off and let the creative juices flow out onto the written page.

Stop when you're ready. This is what's known as a breakthrough, and you've earned it. If your significant other has to pick the kiddies up from Cub Scouts, so be it. If you've got to order Chinese takeout for dinner with your "phone hand" while the other hand flies across the keyboard, all the better.

Just look what you've done. Look what you've accomplished. You've written something. Okay, it could bring you jail time in thirty-eight states, but this is just for you. No one will ever see it, the evidence will be destroyed, and you can do so in an elaborate ceremony by the fireplace to rival those spunky Ya-Ya gals, if you so desire.

The point is, you're back in the saddle again. Congrats!

This is your time to relish what it feels like to be writing again. Just enjoy the feeling and go with it. Don't think that because you can't use this material it's a waste of time; it isn't. You're writing again, and that's what's important.

What to Do When It's a Keeper

"But, Jenna . . . what if I wrote something really, really good and I really, really want to be able to submit it somewhere?" Well then, little camper, it's just going to take a little extra work (or a brilliant lawyer). You have to change the characters' names, obviously, and change anything that came from the original book. For example, if the scene you used as a starting point was about two girls searching for buried treasure, you might want to change it to two boys searching for their kidnapped friend.

You can make this story wholly your own. Using the copied part was just a crutch to get you going, and it is quite possible for you to wind up creating a work that barely relates at all to the original piece if you're willing to rewrite a few times until you've eliminated the traces of your handiwork.

If the block comes back tomorrow, pick up another book and start all over again. Just remember which pages are theirs, and which ones are *yours*.

My writer's block is very logical—it is born of rejection. As a full-time freelance writer, I send out a lot of queries and submissions, and obviously, not all of them are accepted with loving open arms. If the nos come in between the yeses, I carry on unaffected. But when bills pile up, no checks arrive, and rejections come instead, one after the other like the rats in Hamelin, I get writer's block.

It's the child in me throwing a tantrum, I suppose. I recently had a three-rejection day. One arrived by postal mail, another by e-mail in the afternoon, and the last one by e-mail again at night (I thought I'd check my mail one last time before bed, hoping that some good news would help me forget the bad day). I couldn't write or even get ideas for several days.

. . . Until the day I found an article of mine not only accepted, but published on the cover page of the magazine! How the ideas flowed then! Now I'm back in thought and action. I'd better work quickly, before the next batch of rejections arrive . . .

—Hasmita Chander, freelance writer

23

Please, Don't Let This Feeling End

Stopping in Medias Res

Once you get going, it's important not to write all the way to the end of a scene or chapter. Going all the way to the end means you have to start anew the next time you return to your writing; it means you have to stare at that blank page again and figure out how to start a new chapter or scene.

Instead, take a tip from author La'Nelle Gambrell (www.LaNelle.com). "I have a secret," she says. "I always stop in medias res (into the midst of things), sometimes midsentence. If the words are flowing, it's because you know what you want to say, you've already thought things through and you won't (even though you'll think you will) forget them. This is the best time to stop! The words will be there the next day when you go back to work. After I stop writing for the day (stopping in medias res), I try not to think about what I'm writing until I sit back down to work the next day. Honest, you'll pick up right where you left off."

It takes some discipline to work this way. Especially if you're the kind of person who needs closure (like me), it can be difficult to convince yourself to *stop* writing when you're on a roll.

It's the grown-up version of cramming for your high school exams. The old brain is humming, the dialogue is flowing, the characters are meshing, you're firing on all cylinders, and why in the world would you ever want to stop when it just feels so gosh darn good?

You might be tempted to keep typing until you finish "just one more page," or "just this last chapter." The pages pile up, the printer runs out of ink, until your little eyes just can't take it anymore and you finally, finally call it a night.

The problem is that you're leaving yourself at a deficit for the next time. It's like not refilling your car's gas tank at the end of the day when it's on empty. You wake up the next morning, late for work, and you have the unpleasant task of refilling your tank on the way (and coming to the office smelling like a gas station). If you had only left yourself a quarter of a tank or stopped to fill your tank the day before, your day would have started on a completely different note.

Take advantage of the times when the words are flowing freely and quit while you're still excited about what you're writing. Then, the next time you sit down to write, you'll be working off that same energy. You won't have to start on fumes.

If you just can't bear to stop writing, then write notes to yourself instead. Write down the bare essentials of where you want to go with your story, so you'll be absolutely, positively sure to remember.

▶ PROMPT: Pick a nearby object and spend a whole page describing it.

The Muse Within

So much of our writing is magical. Not in the sense that we all write fantasies, mind you, but in the sense that whether we like to admit it or not, we all have a muse helping us fill those pages with lyrics and creativity. And writer's block interrupts that muse, shuts her up, ties her up with a handkerchief, and pushes her down the stairs into the dank, cold basement.

In a way, employing this challenging method of keeping ourselves excited about our writing feels like the same thing. We automatically think: "Wait! What if my muse won't come out tomorrow? What if she thinks I'm being cocky by cutting her off at the knees like this? What if she abandons me for some other writer? One who will keep writing when the spirit strikes? What if she gets hit by a bus? Or gets mugged? Why is she carrying so much cash?"

The fact is, you are your own muse. (You are also very paranoid.) You control when and why you get inspired and, occasionally, even how. You just don't know it. Like all writers, you think there must be something more to it than just some simple schmuck sitting down at a keyboard and making this stuff up. There's got to be some divine intervention, some mythical creature pulling the words out of the fog from Mount Olympus and pushing them through your fingertips.

But you create your own magic, and learning to master the difficult art of keeping yourself excited about your own writing is one way to effectively bottle that magic and keep it stored up for use—when, where, and even how you want to use it.

Rewarding Yourself

Remember to reward yourself, too. I reward myself with toothpaste. (Huh?) It's simple: I don't let myself brush my teeth when I wake up until I've written at least a page. (My cat's the only one around during the day and she has bad breath, too.) You might try a similar reward. Some writers I know don't shower until they've written for an hour. Others splurge on things like fountain pens and eccentric writer wardrobe accessories after a hard day's work.

It is said that the best way to modify behavior is with intermittent rewards—that is, you don't have to go buy yourself a hat every single time you write. It works better when you do it on a semiregular basis.

Stocking Your Savings Account

When you're in a good writing place, take the time to keep your writer's savings account stocked. Most writers I know keep some form of an idea file. This file can take many forms, but I recommend a box of index cards.

On these index cards, you can record bits of conversation, new topics, character descriptions—whatever comes to mind that you want to store for future use. You can even include photos or pictures clipped from magazines.

Some of my best ideas, oddly enough, come when I'm occupying two of the hardest places in which to write: the bed and the bathroom. For just such occasions, I invest in two separate spiral notebooks accompanied by two separate pens, placed just so next to my bed and in a drawer in the bathroom.

Now, when I get a killer idea or brilliant plot twist, out comes one of the notebooks and I jot the idea down before it vanishes into the ether (or before Anthony comes banging on the door). To store the ideas, I take a half hour at the end of each week and convert my notebook ramblings into clearer and more concise sentences on index cards.

Make these cards a priority, for one can never scrimp on ideas. They are the lifeblood of writing and surprisingly taken for granted by today's busy writers with their hectic lives. Dress up your box of index cards with stickers, markers, or pipe clean-ers. Use color-coded cards—red for characters, blue for plot—or even colored ink. Place your box in a prominent spot where you can turn to it quickly and often.

See the cards as an opportunity to explore new avenues, cre-ate new projects, or simply energize a slow writing day when you've run out of coffee. Many of my best ideas—and finished products—have come straight from this box of ideas mas-querading as index cards.

The next time you're experiencing writer's block, you can refer to your index cards as a self-created file of prompts. The cards should spark new ideas for stories and characters.

▶ PROMPT: Finish this sentence in the form of a personal essay: "The hardest lesson I've ever learned was . . ."

Newspaper Inspiration

Another good way to keep your writer's savings account well stocked is to relax with the Sunday paper. Yes, believe it or not, I have discovered a wealth of not only story ideas but paying gigs through leisurely lounging around on a Sunday morning with a full pot of Irish cream coffee and my local paper. Of course, I've got a pad and pen handy for those wonderful ideas, and usually I get pretty close to filling that pad.

"What with?" you might ask. Surprisingly, I start with the lo-cal section. Here I find the latest and greatest news—within a fifteen-mile radius. There are human interest stories I might want to cover, like the senior citizen whose trailer just burned down and is asking for donations, or perhaps I'll turn the story into a Hallmark Hall of Fame script.

Is there a court case I should be covering, either for *True Detective* magazine, Court TV, or my very own true crime book? Or would the paper be more interested in a feel-good story about the new addition to the local humane society? There's no end to the story angles you can find—and pitch—in your local section.

But there's a wealth of other information to be mined from those two pounds of Sunday newsprint as well. Many front pages carry "This Day in History" columns, which can often be quite helpful in researching a current story or perhaps sparking a brand new one. There's always celebrity gossip, which could just fuel a letter to the editor or provide a contact who might buy your next screenplay!

A good way to catalog these ideas—there's nothing worse than being inspired and then losing momentum because you can't find the story idea two weeks later—is to clip them from the paper with a pair of scissors and either tape them to your index cards with relevant notes or start an expandable tickler file full of these bigger, longer, uncut clippings.

Get the idea? From the comics to the recipes, from the coupons to the travel section, you'll find a wealth of inspiration—and caffeination—from your Sunday morning with the paper.

Afterword

You don't need me anymore. Like Christopher Robin outgrew Pooh, you can now safely cast this book aside and get back to what's really important: creating your magic.

You owe it to yourself and the rest of the world to move past the safety net of keeping yourself blocked up (remember: plenty of fiber). It's time to take some real risks and experience the breakthrough that's been patiently waiting for you.

Get back to the thing that initially drew you to writing; indulge your writing fantasies.

Every time we take pen to paper, we have the potential to change the world. Our words may be read in schools two hundred years from now, or they may be read tomorrow by a single woman in another country who just happened to need those words at that moment. Or they may be read only by our friends and family—and that's valuable, too. Maybe our siblings or our old best friend will smile today at a poem we wrote. Maybe that smile was the only bright spot in that person's day.

Writing is a noble profession. Long after we're gone, our words can live on and carry the message of our lives.

What's your message?

Just as you've read mine, I hope that in the not-so-distant future, I will have the pleasure of reading your words as well.

About the Author

Jenna Glatzer is a full-time writer and the editor in chief of Absolute Write (www.absolutewrite.com), a popular on-line magazine for writers. She has hundreds of credits in national print and on-line publications, including *Prevention, Woman's World, Woman's Own, Writer's Digest,* Salon.com, and *Creative Screenwriting,* and she is a many-times optioned and award-winning screenwriter.

She is also the author of several books for children and adults, including *Words You* Thought *You Knew* (Adams Media, fall 2003), and she is the editor of *Conquering Panic and Anxiety Disorders* (Hunter House, 2002), a compilation of success stories from people who have overcome anxiety disorders.

Further, she has a heart-shaped birthmark on her elbow, although it looks more like Florida when she bends her arm.

Index